THE FASTEST
MAN ALIVE

BRIG. GEN. FRANK K. EVEREST, JR., U.S.A.F.
AS TOLD TO JOHN GUENTHER

FOREWORD BY MAJOR GENERAL ALBERT BOYD

BANTAM BOOKS
NEW YORK • TORONTO • LONDON • SYDNEY • AUCKLAND

This edition contains the complete text
of the original hardcover edition.
NOT ONE WORD HAS BEEN OMITTED.

THE FASTEST MAN ALIVE

A Bantam Book / published by arrangement with
the author

PRINTING HISTORY
E.P. Dutton edition published 1958
Bantam edition / August 1990

ISBN 0-553-28771-0

Published simultaneously in the United States and Canada

Bantam Books are published by Bantam Books, a division of Bantam Doubleday
Dell Publishing Group, Inc. Its trademark, consisting of the words ''Bantam
Books'' and the portrayal of a rooster, is Registered in U.S. Patent and Trademark
Office and in other countries. Marca Registrada. Bantam Books, 666 Fifth Avenue,
New York, New York 10103.

PRINTED IN THE UNITED STATES OF AMERICA

OPM   0 9 8 7 6 5 4 3 2 1

"It was a tiny crack in the cockpit canopy, only an inch long . . ."

Remembering all the time, money, and hard work of so many people depending on me, I did not feel the break important enough to call off the flight. The drop and rocket start were clean and quick. Chuck Yeager and Kit Murray were behind me in F-80 chase planes and confirmed that my engine was going.

With three chambers burning I pointed the nose of the X-1 skyward and once more felt the tremendous surge of power thrusting the little airplane into the heavens. In seconds I passed through the buffet region, leveled off and went supersonic, then pulled up again and continued my climb.

Suddenly I heard a loud "poof" in the cockpit and my pressure suit inflated almost simultaneously. In a flash I realized that I had lost cockpit pressure—I saw with a start that the crack had extended and broken completely through. The life-saving pressure of the cockpit had now vanished into the pitiless sky.

Altitude was 65,000 feet. If my pressure suit failed, the rarified air would boil my blood like water . . .

THE BANTAM AIR & SPACE SERIES

To Fly Like the Eagles . . .

It took some 1800 years for mankind to win mastery of a challenging and life-threatening environment—the sea. In just under 70 years we have won mastery of an even more hostile environment—the air. In doing so, we have realized a dream as old as man—to be able to fly.

The Bantam AIR & SPACE series consists of books that focus on the skills of piloting—from the days when the Wright brothers made history at Kitty Hawk to the era of barnstorming daredevils of the sky, through the explosion of technology, design, and flyers that occurred in World War II, and finally to the cool daring of men who first broke the sound barrier, walked the Moon and have lived and worked in space stations—always at high risk, always proving the continued need for their presence and skill.

The AIR & SPACE series will be published once a month as mass market books with special illustrations, and with varying lengths and prices. Aviation enthusiasts would be wise to buy each book as it comes out if they are to collect the complete Library.

DEDICATION

To THE experimental test pilots of America, who flight test new aircraft to the best of their ability, accepting the danger in order that future flights of their fellow pilots will be safer and easier in days to come. They do not wait to be called upon, but volunteer cheerfully for hazardous duty—unswayed by outside persons or pressures, and concerned only with the problems of new and untried planes. Many have made the supreme sacrifice in order that others might live and fly safely. To them and all experimental test pilots who daily risk their lives that aviation may progress, this book is dedicated.

Contents

Note

The following definitions may be helpful to the reader:

Mach (pronounced "mock") number—a measurement of the speed of sound. Mach 1 is the speed of sound, Mach 2 is twice the speed of sound, etc. Speeds less than the speed of sound are expressed as a percentage of Mach number—such as Mach .96. When expressed in knots or miles per hour, the speed of sound varies according to altitude and air temperature. Under average conditions the speed of sound is about 763 miles an hour at sea level.

G—a measurement of the force of gravity acting upon an aircraft in flight. One G is equivalent to the force of gravity, two G's is twice the force of gravity, etc. "Pulling G's" refers to a movement of an aircraft that produces forces greater than the force of gravity. This occurs most commonly in high-speed turns and dives. Both aircraft and crew have limits on the number of G's that they can sustain without harm.

Foreword

Aviation in America has come a long way in a short time. Scarcely fifty years have passed since a directive established on August 1, 1907, an Aviation Division in the Army Signal Corps. From that directive evolved today's United States Air Force.

During this half century, the airplane has reshaped the world, telescoped time, and changed our very way of life. The period has been both dramatic and dynamic. We have progressed from a speed of 30 miles per hour for the Wright brothers Flyer at Kitty Hawk, N.C., to more than 1,900 miles per hour for the Bell X-2 experimental rocket plane.

All this progress has taken place within my lifetime. I was a boy in North Carolina when the airplane—or flying machine, as it was known in those days—first captured the public's imagination. To the thousands of us still active in aviation today, the past half century of aviation is prologue. The great realizations of aviation lie ahead. We have merely skirted the fringes of outer space.

Standing stark against the horizon of yesterday's and today's aviation progress are the test pilots—military and civilian—who daily risk their lives flying untried and experimental planes. Few in numbers, they are members of the world's most exclusive profession—and one of the most dangerous. Their financial reward, modest at best, is hardly sufficient remuneration for the dangers they risk. But these aviation pioneers are charged with courage, and for most of them testing planes is a labor of love.

I am a test pilot myself and I have never known one who was not dedicated to his work. Each in his own way justifies the task to himself with little thought of things monetary. Without them our modern aircraft still would be paper planes on designers' drawing boards. By testing a plane in actual flight, they personally prove its value as an air-borne vehicle.

Lt. Col. Frank K. Everest, Jr. is one of these test pilots—and an excellent one. I met him at Wright Field, Ohio, early in 1946 when he joined my command as a test pilot. I have since followed his career with interest and personal pride in his achievements.

As chief of the Fighter Section at Wright Field and then chief of Flight Test Operations at Edwards Air Force Base, California, Colonel Everest distinguished himself and reflected great and lasting credit on the Air Force through his devotion to duty and his outstanding service and leadership.

Perhaps Colonel Everest's greatest contribution to aviation progress was as an experimental rocket plane pilot. He was one of the Air Force test pilots who flew the Bell X-1 and X-2 experimental rocket planes to new speeds and altitudes.

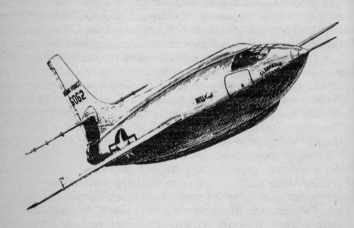

Bell X-1

In flying these supersonic planes, he flew faster and higher than man ever had before.

I am pleased that Colonel Everest has now taken the opportunity presented by this book to report his experiences. It is an important story because his work is important.

Because Colonel Everest is dedicated to his work, aviation and our way of life are richer today. His courage and daring in exploring the frontiers of flight provide us the springboard into the "wild blue yonder" of tomorrow.

ALBERT BOYD
Major General, USAF
Deputy Commander/Weapon Systems

Headquarters, Air Research &
  Development Command
Baltimore, Maryland
  1957

THE FASTEST
MAN ALIVE

Speed Record

"What do you think, Pete?"

George Welch, chief test pilot for North American Aviation Corporation, buckled on his crash helmet and tightened the chin strap. In the brilliant sunlight where we stood outside the aircraft hangar, the cloudless sky arched clear blue over the flat, brown desert floor.

On the concrete apron nearby the two jets waited to take off.

I squinted reflectively into the morning sun, already high in the east. Summer comes soon in Southern California, and now at the end of May the morning was hot despite the early hour.

"I think you can do it, George," I answered. "I think the 100 can do it." I turned and looked again at the shiny new fighter plane, the YF-100 Super Sabre, its glistening aluminum reflecting the sunlight in a thousand crystals.

This was another first time, one of so many we lived with here at Edwards Air Force Base. New planes that had never flown; new speeds and altitudes that had never been reached. Jet engines and rocket engines. Sound barriers and heat barriers. Swept wings and supersonic flight.

I thought for a moment and spoke again. My own helmet was on now, the rubber hose dangling sideways from the open oxygen mask.

"I'll tell you why I think so," I said. "It's because she's got the lines and power to do it. I know it's the first flight for this airplane. I also know that no plane has ever gone supersonic in level flight with a jet engine. So maybe it's unreasonable to expect the 100 to do it the first time up. But I don't agree."

Briefly my mind went back to the Bell X-1 rocket plane and the first supersonic flight, here in the same dry desert six years before. Chuck Yeager, the pilot, was still testing new airplanes here at Edwards. Before he broke the sound barrier, they said he couldn't do it either.

I went on talking.

"There's a first time for everything, including now. I think the 100 has got the stuff, and it doesn't matter that she's never flown before. If the design is right and the power is there, she'll do it any time. And that goes for the first flight too."

"Maybe you're right," George said. We were walking toward the new jet and I waited beside the plane while he climbed up the ladder to the cockpit and eased himself into the seat. He buckled on his safety belt and shoulder harness as he spoke.

"Anyway, we'll soon find out," he grinned down at me. I could see the light in his blue eyes that George always got when he was excited. "Buy you a beer if she does." He leaned down and started the engine and there was a muffled roar as the big J-57 came to life. He was shouting now to make himself heard above the mounting whine of the engine compressor as the speed of the turbine blades increased. "Buy you two beers!"

As he turned and taxied down the concrete strip toward the dry lake bed I walked over to the other jet, ducking to dodge the blast of hot air from his tail pipe. Today I was chase pilot for George as he made the first flight in America's newest and fastest fighter plane. We always flew chase on new and experimental aircraft at Edwards, as one more check of the many we made to see what happened. Chase pilots are useful observers. They are also helpful in getting back safely if something goes wrong.

My jet was an F-86, older and smaller, but still the best in the world in 1953. It held all the official speed records—over 700 miles an hour. It could go supersonic too—in a dive. I did myself, nearly five years earlier, and many more pilots had done so since. But to go supersonic straight and level—no

F-86 Sabre

jet had ever been built with enough power to do that. Not till the F-100, anyway, and its real performance was still unknown. Now we were going to find out.

I buckled myself in my seat and plugged in my oxygen hose. After I started the engine the chocks were removed and I released the brakes. The 86 rolled down the taxi strip onto the lake bed and I took off. George had a couple of taxi runs to make so I was air-borne several minutes ahead of him. As he broke ground I dropped down in position on his wing and called him over the radio. "Turn her loose," I said.

The rapid acceleration of the F-100 left me way behind. George was at 10,000-foot altitude before I got back in formation with him, and then he had to come out of afterburner and throttle back for me to keep up. "She's fast all right," I said to myself. We climbed together to 35,000 feet and leveled off.

I moved in close behind him above and a little to the right. He turned and waved at me through the canopy. "Think she'll fly, George?" I asked him. He came back at once over the radio and his voice sounded happy and excited. "Hang on, here we go," he said.

"Race you!" I retorted. I saw the big hawklike jet lunge forward as he lit the afterburner and grinned despite myself. The 100 was living up to expectations. I threw in full throttle and glanced briefly at my instruments. The needle on the Machmeter crept slowly up to Mach .9 and stopped.

Looking out of the cockpit again, I saw that the F-100 was still accelerating. As I watched, the big jet once more began pulling away from me and dwindled into the distance. Even before George came on the air again I knew what he would say. His voice choked with emotion, he spoke the code word that meant success—"Bingo!" To all who heard him and understood, it said the same thing—this was another first time. Today, for the first time in the annals of aviation history, a jet airplane had gone supersonic straight and level under its own power.

I still had the last word as we turned back toward the dry lake bed far below us. "Okay, two beers," I said.

Two weeks later I took the YF-100 up myself for the first time. By now the Air Force was greatly interested in the fast new jet. Never before had we enjoyed the prospect of a supersonic production aircraft. The only other planes that could match its performance, the rocket-engined Skyrocket and X-1, were experimental research planes, never meant to fly tactical missions. If the 100 worked out, a whole new area of flight would be open to us. In the supersonic regions, where aircraft of no other nation could follow, a new and superior kind of aerial warfare was now possible.

As I released the brakes on the powerful new fighter plane, I could feel the strength of its 10,000 pounds of engine thrust begining to move it along the desert floor. It picked up speed very fast and as I lit the afterburner it broke from the runway far short of the normal take-off run. As it became air-borne I pulled my wheels up, for acceleration was so rapid that I could easily exceed the limit gear speed and pull the gear doors off. Then I pulled the nose up sharply and the airplane shot skyward like a rocket.

This was flying! Except for the experimental X-1, never before had I flown an airplane with comparable performance.

The climb to altitude was short and sweet. At 35,000 feet I leveled off and began accelerating to maximum speed. In brief seconds I saw the jump in the air speed indicator and Machmeter that told me the airplane was supersonic. Now I understood why George Welch had sounded so excited on his first flight. It felt very good to know that this kind of performance was at last available to us.

Other test flights followed that summer, by myself and other military pilots, in an unofficial Air Force evaluation of the new jet. In our eagerness to confirm its apparent superiority, we did not give the manufacturer time to complete his own tests first. Instead we telescoped our evaluations, running both tests simultaneously, impatient to learn any deficiencies that must be corrected before it went into production. We found unstable tendencies at high and low speeds. But we felt that it was basically a good airplane and had good potential, and allowing for necessary changes and modifications before it went into production, we recommended that it be procured for tactical service by the Air Force.

By September George Welch and his test pilots were also satisfied that the F-100 was ready to build. They had completed normal Phase 1 testing and apparently it met its specifications. Among other things, these called for a service ceiling of 50,000 feet and a combat radius of 500 miles. On the strength of their recommendations, as well as our own preliminary evaluations, the F-100 was ordered into production. In the meantime, one of the two prototype airplanes was turned over to us for Phase 2 testing.

Before, we had concentrated on performance. Now for the first time we began testing its handling characteristics—its stability as a gun platform and the effectiveness of its control system under extreme operating conditions. As chief of flight test operations at Edwards, I assigned myself to be the project pilot. In view of the high hopes the Air Force had for this airplane, I wanted to be familiar with its capabilities and shortcomings from firsthand experience. Moreover, I felt an obligation to test the airplane personally; not that my pilots were less capable, but I did not want any blame to fall on others if something went wrong.

As alternate pilot for Phase 2 tests I selected Captain Zeke Hopkins, a former flight test engineer who had only recently joined the operations division. Zeke was a fighter pilot with considerable tactical experience, and with his engineering training he was ideally suited to fly stability and control tests on the new fighter plane. Working as a team, we found many new problems that required corrective action. As a result, our enthusiasm for the F-100 was considerably reduced, and I personally wrote in my report that I thought it should not be released to using commands until the faults had been corrected. In the meantime we continued to test and fly the airplane.

It was generally conceded by Air Force pilots that the Douglas XF4D looked pretty good, especially for a Navy plane. A medium-weight jet fighter, powered by a 10,000-pound thrust engine, the XF4D was considerably faster than previous carrier-based planes. Nicknamed the Skyray because its rounded delta wings resembled the manta ray that lives in the sea, its first public appearance in the summer of 1952 revealed that the Navy was making good progress in aircraft design. While the XF4D was a prototype airplane and a long way from sea duty, it was substantially faster than any production airplane at that time, including our own.

As the Navy had never had a really fast jet fighter such as the F-86, we did not begrudge them a chance to crow a little; all we asked was that they not step on our toes. They had never gone supersonic in their own planes up to this time, borrowing an Air Force jet whenever they wanted to crash the sound barrier, and we actually felt a little sorry for them. Now with the Skyray it looked as though they might have an airplane that could go supersonic in a dive.

We were less understanding, however, when Douglas wheeled out the Y airplane, the second prototype, in October, 1953, and Commander Jimmy Verdon, a Navy test pilot, flew it to a new world's speed record of 753 miles an hour. This was 38 miles an hour better than our own record set earlier that year over the same distance. At this point we stopped feeling sorry for the Navy and started taking stock of ourselves. There were few if any Air Force pilots who could quit work with an easy conscience while the speed record was held by a carrier-based plane.

In the new F-100 we believed we had an airplane that could get the record back. This was for four passes over a

3-kilometer course, a total distance of 7.45 miles. The record had previously been held by two new British jets, the Hawker Hunter and Supermarine Swift with runs of 727 and 735 miles an hour respectively. Under rules laid down by the Fédération Aéronautique Internationale, the world governing body, a new record had to exceed the old record by at least 1 per cent in order to be recognized officially. The F4D beat the best British mark by an ample margin. Now we had to beat the Navy by at least 7½ miles an hour.

This required a speed of at least 761 miles an hour. It would be an average of the four 3-kilometer passes, two each way. North American requested permission to make the attempt and the Air Force approved. As the only Air Force pilot with any large amount of F-100 experience at that time, I was assigned to do the flying.

The next week we took the YF-100 to the Salton Sea, a large inland lake in the Imperial Valley north of the naval air station at El Centro. This was the speed course where the F4D set its record. Good visibility, flat terrain (half the course was over water), and high temperatures made it a superior location for high-speed flights. The National Aeronautic Association sent out official timers from Los Angeles, and North American engineers set up high-speed cameras and electrical timing devices. When they were ready I took the 100 up and flew the course.

I made several flights without getting a record. I was averaging speeds of 754 and 755 miles an hour. This was faster than the F4D, but not 1 per cent faster. Air temperatures were somewhat lower, which reduced my true air speed. If the weather had been warmer I think we could have beaten the Navy record by the required margin.

North American refused to admit it was licked. If the F-100 could not set a speed record on the 3-kilometer course, then they would try the 15-kilometer course, a longer distance but easier to beat. Records over both courses were officially recognized. At that time the 15-kilometer record was only 707 miles an hour, set the previous month by an Air Force F-86. We could beat 707, of course. If we could also surpass the F4D mark by a small margin, North American felt we could then claim the world's record, as there was nothing in the rules that required the 15-kilometer record to exceed the 3-kilometer record by any fixed amount.

We were quite amused by North American's argument, and I personally felt we were not being fair to Douglas and the Navy, who had done a good job with the F4D and deserved the record. To set a new record I thought we should do it over the same distance. But North American was very competitive and insisted on making the effort, so it was agreed to fly the 15-kilometer course.

The course was set up along the eastern shore of the Salton Sea in the Southern California desert. The little town of Thermal, California, was due north. Official timing was with a Speed Graphic Pacemaker camera with Polaroid Land Backs and an electronic counter chronograph accurate to 10 microseconds. The complete panning mechanism was designed and built by North American for the record attempt.

To give me a good landmark, rubber tires were piled 5 kilometers from each end of the course. When ignited they would burn with a heavy black smoke easily visible from a high-speed aircraft in the clear desert air. I would sight along the smoke signals in order to enter the speed traps where the timing mechanism would pick me up at each end of the course. As the first camera hit the 90-degree point it would set off the timing mechanism at the start of my run. The other camera would then pick me up at the far end and pan with me to the end of the course.

On the morning of October 29 I got up early and flew to El Centro in an F-80 jet fighter. North American engineers handling arrangements for the speed run were waiting for me, together with the airplane. Max Wells, the engineer in charge of the project, met me at the field, accompanied by the chief of flight test at North American, George Mellinger. Max called a meeting of everybody concerned with the project, numbering about seventy-five people, and briefed us on the operation of the day.

We were to stand by, starting about 10 A.M., until the temperature reached its maximum. Max figured we would get a half-mile an hour increase in true air speed for every 2-degree rise in air temperature. The timers at the course 30 miles north were alerted by long-distance telephone and the connection kept open, with North American employees taking turns talking so the operator would not disconnect the line. Meanwhile I took the 100 up to make certain it was operating satisfactorily, and I flew a trial run over the course to acquaint myself with the landmarks. After I landed at about 11 o'clock the plane was refueled and there was nothing to do but wait.

The temperature rose as expected until about 1 P.M., when it reached a peak of 85 degrees and started falling. This was the signal to go. Observers and pilots got in the T-28 observation planes and took off. The crash boat proceeded to its station in the Salton Sea a few hundred yards offshore. At the speed course the rubber tires were lit and began sending up thick, black smoke. Trying to hide my excitement, I climbed into the F-100 cockpit and took off.

I planned to stay within 100 feet of the ground on both passes over the 9-mile course. In 1953 we had not perfected timing equipment accurate at higher altitudes. Because I would be flying very fast very near the ground, I knew the air would be choppy and I expected buffeting. For this reason I strapped myself very tightly in my seat.

After the plane was air-borne I cut the afterburner off to conserve fuel for the speed run itself. The fires were going good, and as the first signal came in sight I lined up on the smoke and threw the F-100 to full throttle.

At my request, radio communication was kept at a minimum, but now I broke radio silence. "I'm going to kick her in the tail," I said. With this I cut in the afterburner and the airplane began accelerating up to its maximum speed.

The engine was wide open as I blasted across the starting line and aimed the airplane at the second column of smoke rising in the far distance. Altitude was about 75 feet. Looking down as I flashed past I saw people throw themselves on the ground to escape the shock wave from the airplane. Buffeting was severe as I attempted to maintain a smooth flight path.

I was flying very carefully now. Any slightest forward motion of the stick would take me into the ground in the fraction of a second. Speed was Mach .96. As I hurtled over the second pile of burning tires, I came out of afterburner and began the long, flat turn around to re-enter the traps for my second pass.

FAI rules did not permit runs at over 150 feet or turnarounds over 1,500. This was to prevent diving into the course. In the case of the F-100, however, diving into the course wouldn't help much, because it was up against the maximum drag rise or air resistance, and even if I dove it into the course the plane would drop back to its maximum level flight speed very rapidly.

I entered the traps for my second speed run over a group of houses on the shore of the Salton Sea. I had noticed them on my check flight in the morning and made a mental note to stay clear. We had already had enough complaints about television aerials blown down and windows broken by shock waves from previous flights. But despite all I could do I had to fly very close to them to hold my altitude at the predetermined limits.

The airplane began buffeting again from rough air as I started my second pass over the marked course. Speed was slightly slower because of the head wind but I thought my average would still be high enough to set a new record. Then I was over the far end and out of the traps. I pulled up sharply

F-80 Shooting Star

to gain altitude, flipped over in a few victory rolls and headed for El Centro.

In a few minutes George Mellinger phoned from Thermal with the welcome news that the unofficial figures looked good. With nothing to do but wait, I got in my F-80 and flew to Thermal Airport where the timers were reducing the data and getting the corrected figures. About 7 o'clock Bertrand Rhine of the NAA told me I had a new record.

The average of both passes was slightly over 755 miles an hour. This was only two miles an hour faster than the Navy's record, but still good enough to be official. Under Fédération Aéronautique rules, the fastest average for either distance is recognized as the world's record. Rhine said he would submit my mark for official recognition, which he did. I had hoped to beat the Navy by 1 per cent, but with the lower temperatures during my flight this was not possible. I offered to try again, but North American was satisfied; the F-100 was now the fastest plane in the world.

In the four years since that time, my record has been broken by other pilots. In 1955 and again in 1956 newer models and other planes were flown faster. But mine was the last record flown close to the ground. Perfection of new high-altitude timing equipment has made it unnecessary to repeat the hazardous low-altitude speed runs. The first man to break my record two years later flew at 35,000 feet, with no danger of flying into the ground. In thinner air at high altitudes airplanes can also fly faster. With our present supersonic aircraft, of course, official speed records are meaningless; today test pilots at Edwards Air Force Base break the existing world's record every day of the week.

On returning to Edwards I found trouble brewing. North American Aviation took exception to my negative report on the F-100 and assured Air Force Headquarters that the airplane was safe to fly. George Welch stated that the 100 was one of the easiest and nicest airplanes he had ever flown.

Back at Edwards, I had another fight on my hands. Although my own pilots supported me, other officers felt I might be mistaken, so it was suggested that the F-100 be flown and tested by squadron pilots from the Tactical Air Command.

Used to flying earlier jets, they were much impressed by the superior performance of the 100 and praised it in glowing terms. Unfortunately, they lacked the opportunity to fly it long enough to learn its shortcomings. They too felt it was ready for tactical service. Later on, when I was called back to Washington to defend my recommendations in person they testified that they had not encountered any trouble at all. The only complaint they had was that the airplane was not fast enough.

Confronted with these expert opinions from both the manufacturer and our own tactical pilots, Headquarters ruled that the F-100 would be continued in production. Many months later, after airplanes had been delivered and released to using commands, my warnings unfortunately came true. There were four major F-100 accidents, including two pilots killed. One was my good friend George Welch. He was killed near Edwards while making a structural demonstration dive test to pull maximum design G's on the airplane at maximum speed and Mach number.

He had made one flight in the morning, but because he encountered difficulty in diving the F-100 to its maximum speed at the right altitude, he was able to get only about 6½ G's in his dive.

On his second flight he reached the limit dive speed and pulled back hard on the stick. Apparently he pulled only 6½ G's again, and noting this he jerked the stick back even farther. Records recovered from the airplane showed there was a noticeable yawing moment as he did so, or sideward movement of the tail, and as the G's increased the yawing moment increased too.

The records indicated that he exceeded 7.33 G's, pulling slightly more than 8 G's on the airplane, and at the same time the yaw angle suddenly increased, first to 15 degrees and then completely off the record. The F-100 was built to withstand only 8 degrees of yaw at maximum speed before structural failure, and when the airplane reached this high yaw angle either the nose section or tail came off and the airplane disintegrated.

As a result of this and other accidents, resulting from the airplane's lack of directional stability, all F-100's were returned to the manufacturer for costly and time-consuming modifications. The problem was not corrected without a major design change requiring a larger vertical fin on the stabilizer. It was several years after the problem was discovered that the F-100 was at last ready for unrestricted use. Today, of course, it is considered to be a safe and acceptable airplane, and I think it is the best tactical fighter in service at this writing.

It is not my purpose in telling this story either to criticize or condemn. These men were my friends and we disagreed honestly. Rather it is my hope that it will contribute to a better understanding of the need for flight testing. It has not been many years since all testing was done by manufacturers. Only since World War II has the Air Force tested its own planes. But in one short decade the military test pilot has proved the value of his contribution. Working closely with one another, military and civilian test pilots are giving us better and safer airplanes.

Although I have left flight testing, the story of the F-100 has not ended for me. Today I command a Super Sabre squadron in Europe. As an F-100 pilot, I am reminded every day of the importance of flight testing. For some other test pilot would have found the problem had I not done so. And I can fly with more confidence because I know the 100 is a good airplane. So it is today with all Air Force planes and pilots. Perhaps that is the greatest contribution of flight testing.

2

Pilot

"Pete?"

"Yes, Mom."

"Where are you?"

"Out in back watching an airplane."

In the kitchen of the nearby house, I heard her turn and speak to my father, who was enjoying a late Saturday morning breakfast.

"I declare, Ken, I don't know what's got into that boy. I told him to cut the grass an hour ago, and instead he's out there lying in it. Next thing we know he'll be flying."

I was born in 1920 at Fairmont, a small industrial town on the steep banks of the Monongahela River in the hill country of northern West Virginia. My father was Frank Kendall Everest, an electrician who came to Fairmont from Ohio. My mother was Phyllis Walker, a schoolteacher. Dad's parents emigrated to America from Peterborough, in England. Mother's people have always lived around Fairmont. On her mother's side, the Hayhursts, they go back to the early settlers who came to America from England with William Penn.

I grew up in the hills. Our first house was a white frame cottage in Hillcrest, a suburb on the edge of town. When I was five years old we built a new house in Forest Hills, nearer to town. It is the highest point in Fairmont and has a fine view for miles around.

My first school was a small red schoolhouse about a mile

from home. I liked my teachers and playmates and was eager
to learn. After school and on holidays I played in the mead-
ows surrounding our house. When I was a child we had few
neighbors, so I was alone much of the time. I became expert
with a slingshot and spent many solitary hours outdoors
hunting birds and small game in the fields and woods.

Possibly because of my lonely childhood, I later found it
hard to come forward and be friendly—it was difficult for me
to do and still is. Even today I find it hard to join a group I
don't know and mix well with them. But once the ice is
broken I feel free and less reserved, and I have a real warm
association with people I know and like. When I make a
friend I keep him.

As far back as I can remember, I always wanted to go fast.
I got my first bicycle when I was ten and would ride it down
the hill without touching the brakes. It was the same way
rollerskating and riding sleds. In those days cars were few,
and you could slide all the way to the bottom of the hill
without stopping. At the end of the road was a highway with
more traffic but I never stopped until the last moment. I could
always go faster on a bicycle too because of the chances I
took.

Although I was small as a boy, I was cocky and liked to
fight. But despite my eagerness, my size was against me, and
in scraps with bigger boys I took many a licking. As I grew
older I took up boxing and wrestling in school and won most
of my bouts when I was matched with someone my own size.
Later on I participated in group sports and enjoyed them
primarily because I like competition.

As a boy I went to Sunday school at the First Methodist
Church in Fairmont. Later I joined the boys' choir at the
Christ Episcopal Church. My mother was a pianist and liked
music, and she encouraged my singing. One day Rev.
Brickman, the pastor and choirmaster, called me in after
rehearsals and excused me from further sessions, explaining
that my voice was changing. I was sorry, because I enjoyed
choir work and liked to sing.

When I was ten years old I saw my first airplane. It was
early June, the grass in the back yard was green and inviting,
and instead of cutting it I preferred to lie in it. I was stretched
out on the ground, daydreaming as boys will do, when the

sound of an engine roused me. Opening my eyes I looked up and saw a little Curtiss Jenny flying lazily overhead. As I watched fascinated the pilot began his stunts.

First a few slow rolls, then some loops and Immelmanns, and finally a couple of spins. As I admired the easy grace and movement of the little biplane, I was aware of a new and strange desire to be up in the sky myself. The pilot, a stunt flier from Morgantown, was later killed putting on an air show. But seeing him that day more or less decided me on my future ambitions. From that time on my whole goal was to learn to fly and become a pilot myself.

Several years passed before I took my first airplane ride in an old Ford Trimotor, flown by another barnstormer from a cow pasture near my home. I was thrilled being up in the air, high over the city, looking down at people and having a feeling of freedom from all things earthly. Although I was still a youth, this experience confirmed my early desire to be an aviator. When I was old enough to fly I took the first opportunity to learn and never changed my mind.

My parents were happily married and I had a fond relationship with both of them; but being stubborn and independent, I usually tried to work out my own problems. Dad was often in the background, mother being the stronger-minded of the two, and she exerted the disciplinary action. Severe corporal punishment mother turned over to Dad, but as for other punishment requiring the use of the tongue, she was more than capable of doing that herself.

It was mother who saw to it that I stuck to my studies and learned how to behave properly, teaching me the manners used in that area in those days. It was she who kept me on the right path and directed my efforts. Dad was busy working during the day, of course, and naturally he spent less time at home, but he liked hunting and fishing, and taught me those sports, as well as others that we shared together during my early life.

When I was a boy, there was a lot of new construction in Fairmont, and my father's work grew to the point where he opened his own business as an electrical contractor. But as with many others, things were slow for him during the depression in the 1930's. Twice during this period we moved away from Fairmont when he took work in other cities, renting our home both times.

We spent one year at Long Branch, New Jersey, where Dad had a contract to wire the barracks at Fort Monmouth. We spent another year in Alexandria, Virginia, near Washington, when he got a contract to wire new quarters at Fort Belvoir. I had a paper route to help out and made about two dollars a week, which I used to buy my own clothes and the luxuries of life important to a boy fifteen years old.

It was in Alexandria that I taught myself to drive a car, taking the keys from Dad's dresser one evening and making my solo in his 1928 model-A Ford. During the next few weeks I sneaked the car out again several times and drove it around the block, going farther as I grew bolder and gained experience. When Dad finally caught up with me I got a good thrashing, as I was too young to drive legally and did not have a license.

When we returned to West Virginia I gladly rejoined my old classmates and friends who were now in high school. In particular I looked forward to seeing my Fairmont girl friend. But she had found new beaux in my absence and was not interested in me any longer. This was my first case of broken love and my feelings were hurt for a few days. I was just an average student in high school. Things that interested me I did well— foundry, machine shop, and mechanical drawing. I grasped things easily but did not take the time or have the patience to apply myself. As a result, I got poor grades in classes that did not interest me, and although I had always read a lot, things like English and history were probably my worst subjects.

When I reached my sixteenth birthday Dad let me get my first driver's license. He also gave me permission to use the family car, another secondhand Ford, on special occasions. My love of speed again asserted itself, and I began driving fast for thrills. I had several automobile accidents while in high school, damaging the car on each occasion, but without injury to myself or others. I also set several speed records between Fairmont and neighboring towns.

Racing against time over hills and on winding roads, I averaged 60 miles an hour to places like Clarksburg, Grafton, and Morgantown. Looking back on those days, I realize it was extremely hazardous driving light stock cars at excessive speeds on ungraded curves, but we considered it an accomplishment to beat existing records for the distances, and I took the chance. If there had been so-called "hot rods" available to me I would probably have tried to go even faster.

Like most boys of my age, I enjoyed the company of girls and had one or two serious romances, but none lasted very long. Mostly I dated different girls, and no single one for any length of time. One of these girls was Avis Mason, who later became my wife.

She was small and very pretty, with wavy brown hair, a good mind, and a sense of humor. I knew Avis in school but we were in different classes, so we didn't get acquainted for some time. Our affair really began at a birthday party at her home. It wasn't a very happy evening for me at first, as the car got stuck on the way over, and by the time I got back on the pavement my clothes were covered with mud. This was quite embarrassing to me, but Avis laughed it off, which made me feel better, and I thought she was a good sport and would be fun to be with.

After that I used to see her at the local night spot, the Fireside Inn, and would dance with her now and then. She was an outstanding dancer and I enjoyed dancing too, so we began dating. There wasn't much affection for the first few months, as it was dancing that brought us together rather than any romantic attraction. But as we grew to know each other we found more things in common, and after a while we fell in love.

Her mother was very upset when Avis became serious about me; she thought I was too wild, and tried to break up our courtship. She even forbade Avis to date me, but when this happened I usually got a friend to stand in. Avis came out of the house with the other boy and we would then switch dates until the evening was over, when he would take her home again.

Along with my dating and fast driving, I was also interested in sports. I played intramural football in high school and was a member of the swimming team. I was too light for varsity football, weighing around 120 pounds, but despite my size I was a good quarterback and played many sandlot games. I went out for the freshman team in college but hurt my knee in practice and had to quit for the season.

I finished high school in 1938 and entered Fairmont State Teachers College, located on another hill near my home. I spent a year studying science and liberal arts and working for my father on weekends. Dad wanted me to be an electrical engineer, and I would have remained in Fairmont and gone into business with him had I not become an aviator. But I was only nineteen at the time, still looking for a thrill, and it was not in me to settle down and sit quietly at home. I still wanted to fly airplanes, and the upshot was that I applied for cadet training in the Army Air Corps.

I took the written examinations at Wright Field, at Dayton, Ohio, and went home to await the results. The Army turned me down. The subjects covered demanded a college training, with heavy emphasis on mathematics and science, and I didn't have enough education to pass the tests. They would take me without an examination if I got two years of college credits in the right subjects, but this meant going back to school and taking more engineering. Since I could not get it at Fairmont State Teachers College, I transferred to West Virginia University in Morgantown.

War began in faroff Europe that fall. There was no reason to believe that our country would become involved—in fact the leaders in Washington were busy telling us we would stay out. But with my plans to become an Army aviator, I heard the war news with more than average interest, feeling that I myself might someday be fighting in the skies over Europe.

Winter in Morgantown is not usually an attractive season, and this year was no exception. Bleak skies, raw winds, and cold rain kept my spirits below normal. Unable to afford a fraternity, I lived in a cheap boardinghouse and worked on weekends to help pay my expenses, with about fifty cents a day left over for spending money. At school I found engineering classes a little tougher than what I had been used to. The combination of all these things, together with being away from home and living in strange surroundings, left me lonely and unhappy.

Under the circumstances, it is perhaps little wonder that I quit school at the end of the first semester. Looking back on it now, I realize that this was a mistake which could have had serious results, because it might have kept me out of cadet training permanently. But at the time I was irresponsible and easily discouraged.

With Dave Thompson, a boyhood friend who became a Navy pilot, I thumbed my way to Florida, where we found work as dishwashers in a hotel at Coral Gables. I think this experience shook me up and brought me to my senses. After two months scrubbing dirty dishes, I realized there was no future for me in the hotel business. Dave was a silverware man, which was considered to be a better job, but apparently he arrived at the same conclusion. At any rate, when some friendly hotel guests offered to drive us to Washington on their way back north, we both accepted gladly. I went back to work for Dad and in the fall of 1940 returned to my engineering studies at Morgantown.

School found me in an entirely different frame of mind. Instead of disliking it, now I was impatient to go ahead and get it over with, in order to qualify for flying training. School itself was only a means to this end. I had no desire to acquire a formal education in engineering or any other profession. One more semester of credits would be enough to meet my cadet requirements, and this was my sole objective.

But war in Europe, which still seemed far away, was bringing me closer to flying than I had dreamed of a year earlier. As a result of the Nazi conquest of Europe, the federal government set up a new civilian pilot training program at selected colleges and universities. Under this program, training facilities were provided by the school and students could learn to fly at government expense. West Virginia University was one of the schools selected for pilot training and I was admitted to the first class.

Morgantown airport was built in 1935 as a work-relief project of the U.S. government during the business depression. It was a bleak deserted field, made by knocking off the top of a West Virginia hill. On this site were built two dirt strips each 3,600 feet long set in an X-shape on the weed-infested ground. Because of light traffic, commercial business was poor, and the new airport did not attract much airline service; however, private flying became popular in Morgantown and several charter services were organized to rent light planes and make local flights.

One of these was the Pioneer Flying Service, owned and operated by Ralph ("Jelly") Boone, a local flyer and businessman. He was a big jolly fellow, well liked by both his customers and business associates. When the CPT civilian pilot training program got under way at West Virginia University, Boone's firm was selected to conduct it.

The course consisted of thirty hours of primary instruction in J-2 Piper Cubs and twenty hours of secondary in Wacos and Stearmans. Small, light, and very slow, these were well-known training planes of the day. The first CPT class at Morgantown consisted of fifteen students, divided into three sections for instructional purposes. The instructor for my section was A. W. ("Snuffy") Smith.

He came from Pittsburgh, where he had worked as a newspaper and magazine distributor, and had learned to fly at Morgantown. A quiet, reserved man, "Snuffy" was an excellent instructor. When war began he went to Lakeland, Florida, as a civilian instructor at a naval flying school, and after the war took a job with the U.S. Weather Bureau at Lakeland.

Manager of the airport was Lee Rennick, a bluff, hearty man who is still on the job today. He made his office on the edge of the field in an abandoned streetcar, which was heated in cold weather by an old-fashioned coal-burning stove. During my student days at Morgantown, we often came in from flying to warm ourselves around the potbellied stove and spent many happy hours in hangar flying.

The J-2 Cub was a typical training plane of the day. It had a 55-horsepower engine with which it took off and landed at about forty miles an hour. I sat in the rear seat behind the instructor. As I was small in stature I couldn't see too well during landings, but managed to avoid any accidents. The plane did not have any brakes, and when it landed you waited for the tail skid to slow it down while you kept it straight on the runway with the rudder pedals.

I received my first flying lesson in December, and from that day on I lived only to fly. Academic subjects became a necessary evil, something to be endured until the end of classes each afternoon when I was free to go to the airport. I even gave up weekend work, gladly sacrificing the extra money just to hang around the airport. I flew at every opportunity in any kind of weather. On many days I would be up flying with a head cold and with feet half-frozen, but heedless of aches and pains and winter weather. Nothing could keep me from a lesson. Even when I wasn't scheduled to fly, most of my free time found me at the field.

When I took off I felt that I was part of the airplane, and once air-borne I forgot everything else and the little Cub became my whole life. I concentrated on flying to the exclusion of all else. As a result, my aptitude was above average and my enthusiasm was unlimited. In any line of endeavor, people will be good at things they like to do, and I loved to fly.

After several hours of dual instruction, "Snuffy" took me up once more and asked me to land the plane. My performance did not satisfy him, however, and we went around and shot several more landings. It was a cold windy day with snow and ice on the ground. After finally coming down I was numb from the cold and looked forward to going inside and getting warm. But before I could shut down the engine, "Snuffy" climbed out and turned around.

"You go on and take it around the pattern a few times," he said.

I was a little awestruck, as I had not expected to solo at this time. I felt choked with emotion and my heart came up in my throat. Then I taxied out and took off and flew around for a while and it was the grandest feeling in the world. All the numbness from being cold and tired went away, and I became quite warm and happy. I shot two or three landings to stay aloft as long as possible, then landed and taxied back to the hangar.

In February I completed the secondary instruction and got my private license. The semester ended a few days later and I transferred back to Fairmont State Teachers College. I now had the engineering credits I needed to apply for aviation cadet training and there was no longer any need to live away from home. In the meantime, I continued my studies in science and general subjects. I still returned to Morgantown occasionally to fly on weekends, but the planes were expensive. Consequently I flew only half a dozen times after my CPT course was completed. As much as I enjoyed it, flying was still a luxury for me and had to wait.

When school was out in June, I immediately applied for aviation cadet training and the Army called me to take my physical examination in August. Two months of fretting and waiting passed before I knew the results. In October word finally came that I was accepted and telling me to report for induction at Columbus, Ohio. On November 9 I was sworn in and left by train for Kelly Field at San Antonio, Texas.

Avis Mason was still my best girl. Ours had been an on-again, off-again kind of romance, with a college-days engagement punctuated by disagreements and lovers' spats. For the past year Avis had represented a kind of conflict in my mind. Flying was my life and I knew it would be impossible for me to give it up. Sometimes I feared that it would be hard for Avis to have an aviator as a husband. After I applied for cadet training, however, we talked seriously about getting married when I was commissioned in the Army, and though I feel she thought it would never happen, she agreed to marry me after I graduated.

Avis knew how vitally important flying was to me. I had often explained to her that I was so constituted that I would have to do everything I could to fly, and go places, and do whatever my service duties required. I have often marveled at the understanding with which Avis accepted this before we were married, as she has since. Apparently she felt there need not be any serious conflict, and so it has worked out. She has never worried much about my flying, and we have never disagreed about it. Her confidence and support have meant more to me than I can express.

After six weeks in the replacement depot at Kelly Field receiving basic military training, I was ordered to primary flying school at Sikeston, Missouri, near St. Louis. This was a civilian school conducted under military contract. The airfield was a rolling meadow with dirt runways, much like Morgantown airport where I had learned to fly the previous winter. The planes were much alike too. I began dual instruction in the Fairchild PT-19 trainer, a low-wing monoplane with a Ranger engine, soon followed by the Stearman PT-18 biplane. After a dozen flights I soloed the Stearman on January 11. In the next few days I flew several times to nearby fields and returned to Sikeston alone.

My parents brought Avis down after Christmas and we formalized our engagement. I bought her engagement ring and we chose our bands for a double-ring wedding. From

Sikeston I entered basic flight training at Randolph Field, Texas. As headquarters of the Army Air Corps at that time it was known as the West Point of the Air; and by comparison with the cold weather and makeshift quarters at Sikeston, the warm climate and comfortable barracks at Randolph Field seemed like luxury.

I began flying a new airplane, the North American BT-14 basic trainer with a Pratt & Whitney engine. It developed 450 horsepower, considerably more than planes I had flown previously, and of course had much higher performance. For the first time I also took lessons from military instructors. After half a dozen flights I soloed the BT-14 without much difficulty. I became proficient in acrobatic flying and could do rolls and loops better than my instructor. It was at Randolph that I learned the basic fundamentals of military flying.

We flew formation, an essential in combat; instrument flying under the hood, another military essential; and radio navigation and night flying. As my skill increased and I gained confidence, my early enthusiasm for aviation continued to grow. It seemed to me that I was born to fly. This was what I wanted; there was no more playing around. I found cadet life a great pleasure and enjoyed every moment of those early days. The three months I spent at Randolph Field were deeply fulfilling and rewarding.

From Randolph I was sent to Foster Field, Texas, in May, for advanced training. Here we were graduated to another new plane, the North American AT-6, another low-wing monoplane with still higher performance. I soloed after one flight and buckled down to completing my training.

We flew at all hours of the day and night—cross-country, instrument and formation flying, night flights, acrobatics, and simulated combat. I especially liked the gunnery training on the Gulf of Mexico. For two weeks we lived in tents, flew in shorts off sand runways, and fired live ammunition. I was just an average gunner, which was disappointing to me. However, I became very adept at formation flying and aerial maneuvers. At the end of June I returned to Foster Field and completed my training.

During the last month of school, Avis and I confirmed our plans to marry after my graduation. In preparation for the wedding, I asked Dave Thompson to stand up for me; but he had enlisted in the Royal Canadian Air Force and wrote back not to plan on him, as he wasn't sure he could get leave. As a substitute I asked Raymond Closson, another Fairmont friend, to do the honors; but Ray was in the infantry at Fort Benning by now and gave me the same answer. In desperation I wrote to a third friend, John Jones, who was still in Fairmont; to my great relief he assured me he would be happy to act as best man.

On July 3 I received my commission as a second lieutenant in the Army Air Corps assigned to fighters. I drove home in a car pool and we were married on July 8. I had two best men; Dave and John both showed up for the wedding. As a result of an automobile accident the previous autumn, I was without a driver's license, and Avis didn't have one; but my cousin Ed Lively and his new bride kindly drove us to our honeymoon hotel in the mountains and brought us home. I was happy, but flying was still most important to me. Even before we got back I was impatient to begin fighter training and go overseas.

After home leave I reported to my outfit at Baltimore, Maryland, Municipal Airport. It was the 314th Fighter Squadron of the 324th Fighter Group, with group headquarters also located at Baltimore. I found a room for Avis and myself and drove to the field every morning with a classmate from cadet school, James Whiting.

Our squadron was flying the Curtiss-Wright P-40, a low-wing monoplane armed with six .50-caliber machine guns. Although it was quite heavy, weighing 8,800 pounds, it was reputed to be very fast for that time, and I looked forward to flying it with some apprehension. I liked the performance but I had never flown an airplane capable of doing 400 miles an hour. When we were ordered to check out in it at Washington National Airport where the runways were longer, this confirmed my opinion that the P-40 must be a champion.

As I started the Rolls-Royce-Packard engine and taxied out to the end of the runway, the noise it made and the feeling of power it gave the airplane left no doubt in my mind that this was a supership. Certain it would accelerate so rapidly that my head would snap backward, I placed my head against the crash pad behind the pilot's seat. Then I applied full throttle and held my breath.

P-40

As the P-40 moved sluggishly down the runway, I thought something must be wrong with the engine. No fighter plane could act like this! But the engine was putting out all the power it had, and after staggering down the length of the field, I finally became air-borne. I went out of sight of the field before I dared pull up the landing gear, barely able to maintain flying speed at 120 miles an hour. With gear up I was able to go a little faster but top speed that day was far below 400. I flew P-40's for the next two years on more than a hundred combat missions, but for me it never did measure up.

After transition to P-40's we returned to Baltimore, where we continued fighter training, at the same time standing alerts for air defense of the East Coast. Our group worked under the Philadelphia air control center, commanded by Colonel Pete Quesada, who later went to England and led the Ninth Fighter Command during the invasion. When alerted by telephone, we took off to intercept and identify unknown planes, which always turned out to be other military aircraft or commercial airliners.

We flew constantly all fall, rotating operations between Baltimore and Bolling Field outside of Washington, with a week in each place. Lt. Robert F. Worley, our squadron commander, liked to fly as much as I did, and we struck up a lasting friendship. When he went up he would often request that I fly his wing, and we flew many times in formation. He took a liking to my ability and I returned his esteem.

I liked to fly and was always available. In three and a half months I flew 150 hours, more than double the squadron average. With this experience I developed extra proficiency in P-40 operations. I was standing alert as a flight leader in those days, and whoever flew with me had to keep pace. I was very definite on my take-offs; I took the airplane off the ground as soon as it developed flying speed and pulled the gear up immediately. After becoming air-borne I dropped my left wingtip and began my turn out of the pattern, almost dragging the wing on the ground. On landing I could three-point it in anywhere I wanted. Because of my enthusiasm and proficiency, I was promoted to first lieutenant four months after graduation.

Avis found Baltimore considerably less exciting; life in a rented room was confining and dull. Usually she got out with other wives during the day for shopping or movies. Sometimes there were dances or parties in the evening, but the pilots worked hard during the duty hours, and our social life suffered as a result.

I think we were both ready to leave when my orders came to prepare for overseas movement. For Avis, it meant going home to Fairmont and long, anxious months of waiting. For me it was an exuberant feeling of knowing that I would soon meet the test of combat—the supreme gamble, with my life itself at stake. I wanted to get into combat. The P-40 wasn't the best airplane for the job, but it was the only one available to me and it would have to do.

3

Combat

Group and squadron headquarters were established overseas in Egypt early in January, 1943. Our first base was Landing Ground 91, a temporary airstrip in the desert near Alexandria. By now our planes were beginning to catch up with us, and upon the arrival of advance elements of our ground echelon from the States, we began to do some flying. We lived in tents and ate British rations; everything was in short supply, and the weather was cold, wet, and windy. But life improved when we moved next month to a permanent field at Kabrit. Weather and housing were better and we immediately launched upon intensive training for combat.

Our group was assigned to the United States Ninth Air Force, which was supporting the British Eighth Army commanded by General Montgomery. Victorious over the Nazi Afrika Korps at El Alamein in Egypt, he was now pursuing the Germans under Field Marshal Rommel westward along the Mediterranean. Both British and American planes flew air support for the Desert Rats as they drove the enemy across Africa. After a month at Kabrit, enough ground echelon was available to maintain one squadron, and early in March we were ordered into combat.

This was my squadron, the 314th. For purposes of organization and operations we were attached to the 57th Fighter Group, a P-40 outfit based at Ben Gardan in eastern Tunisia, several hundred miles west. With Bob Worley, our squadron commander, in the lead, our twelve planes took off from

Kabrit airfield early on the morning of March 8 and headed for the front.

Flying over Egypt and Libya with five stops en route, we reached Ben Gardan on the second day and prepared to go operational. For the first time I got the smell of war. The battlefront was only a few miles ahead on the road to Medenine, a highway junction near the coast. We bedded down for the night beside slit trenches under a strict blackout; our planes often raided the German airfields under cover of darkness and the Jerries were known to reciprocate. The next day we flew a training mission and there was another training flight the following morning. In the afternoon all four squadrons went up on a fighter sweep looking for trouble.

In the air we formed in flights of four planes each and headed north along the coast. I was flying wing to my flight leader, Pete Simpson, who was flying element with one of the squadron commanders of 57th Group. Our objective was the little port city of Gabes less than a hundred miles distant. We expected to meet the Jerries on the way, and we were also looking for targets of opportunity on the ground.

Approaching Gabes we were jumped by thirty German fighter planes, the fast little Messerschmitt 109's. This was the combat I wanted! A 109 diving out of the sun put a 20-millimeter cannon shell in front of me and Pete Simpson's P-40 coughed black smoke and spun earthward. Another 109 above and behind me knocked out my radio. Without a flight leader or radio communications, I yanked the nose up in a steep climb, seeking the comparative safety of altitude. The air was filled with careening planes as individual dogfights raged all about me. Then suddenly I was above and beyond the melee, out of contact with the enemy and all alone.

Looking down I could see Gabes far below, and as I watched the antiaircraft batteries in the little city got my range. The black smoke from the exploding 88-millimeter shells walked across the sky in front of me, like puffs of black cotton in the clear air. Very deliberately I found myself flying from puff to puff along the bursts of flack, absurdly confident that lightning would not strike twice in the same place that day. Then I was out of range of the guns and the planes were gone. With the sky over the blue ocean once more empty and silent, I turned and headed soberly for home.

We moved up as the front moved back, following the retreating enemy along the Tunisian shore. Through March and April we flew almost daily out of new airstrips on the road to Gabes and beyond. From the port cities ahead of us, the Nazis were leaving Africa almost under our guns. Ships and planes plied the strait of Sicily as Rommel attempted to evacuate the remnants of his invading army from their African debacle. Mostly the Germans traveled under cover of darkness, but in daylight hours we struck at everything that moved.

Across the Gulf of Gabes now, and north, in the middle of April we moved once more to El Jemm on the road to Tunis only a hundred miles away. We were tired, hot, and thirsty, but we had orders to press the attack, and after refueling we took off on a late patrol.

All four squadrons were up again, forty-eight aircraft in all, with ten Royal Air Force Spitfires from the 244th Fighter Wing flying top cover. Altitude was about 10,000 feet as we headed northeast over the Mediterranean toward the German shipping lanes. Night was coming and we figured the Jerries would be on the move once more; there was still light enough to see them and after that things wouldn't take very long.

The cry "Enemy aircraft below!" over my radio snapped me to attention. Leaning to the right in the cockpit, I peered down toward the shadowy water, and far below, flying almost on the surface, droned the dark V's of a hundred German transport aircraft bound for Sicily. From our altitude 2 miles up, the big Junkers looked like specks on the ocean. Then the radio crackled with commands and I turned the nose of my P-40 downward as the group peeled off for the kill.

As we dove unerringly toward the packed troop transports now doomed to destruction, again my radio headset filled with alerts. Now they came from our top cover of Spitfires patrolling above us. "Enemy aircraft high!" was the cry this time, and glancing up momentarily, I saw fifty ME-109's diving through the Spitfires toward our formation.

Once more the air filled with swirling and falling planes. Outnumbered though they were, the RAF boys were hot on the heels of the Jerries, flashes of flame from their tracer bullets lighting up the gathering dusk. Our group held our course steadily downward, the whine of the airflow rising in pitch over the cockpit as our dive momentum increased.

Now! I thought. I squeezed the trigger at the lumbering Junkers lined up in my gunsights and felt the P-40 tremble as six guns fired in unison. Then I pulled up sharply a few feet above the water, the G's mounting in my body from the sudden deceleration, and looking back I saw the big transport plane fall flaming into the sea.

Leveling off again, I saw another Junkers transport ahead of me and a little to the right, and automatically I turned slightly to line him up and squeezed my guns. I saw my tracer bullets hit him in the left wing and engine, and even as I watched, the ruptured fuel tanks burst into orange fire and the crippled transport veered helplessly into the ocean and cartwheeled over on its back.

I shook my head to clear the mists that obscured my vision for a moment. Then I looked around for friendly aircraft and saw a sky filled with burning and falling planes. Below me the surface of the sea was dotted with smouldering wreckage and drifting smoke. Most of the German transports had gone.

Some of our boys were turning back to engage the Messerschmitts, and with the Spitfires also after them, the battle was mostly above me now. As I began climbing to join the fray, in the distance I saw a single transport low above the water, flying alone in an effort to escape. I turned into him broadside and fired as I turned, observing my bullets strike his fuselage amidships behind the wings. At that instant I felt the stick tremble and my plane nosed down briefly. As I attempted to pull up again I found that the elevator was responding sluggishly. Looking back, I saw my left stabilizer was blown off, and above me a 109 was turning into position for another shot.

Realizing my helpless predicament, I pulled the control stick back as hard as I could. All thoughts of the Junkers were forgotten; my only thought now was to turn inside the 109. As I fought the controls desperately, the plane slowly responded and began turning. Then I looked around again for my attacker but in the swirling melee and gathering darkness he was gone.

Darkness saved me. I turned southwest, away from the battle, and in a minute it was behind me. Now I saw other

P-40's limping homeward, one by one. We grouped together in a loose formation, more for company than anything else, and set our course for the El Jemm airfield. Soon the darker color of the earth below told us we were over land again, and a few miles farther on we saw through the shadows of evening the sandswept runways that were home.

From El Jemm we moved at the end of April to Qairouan, 50 miles below Tunis, where we flew combat missions for another thirty days. The German Air Force had pulled back to Sicily and Italy and most of our work was strafing and dive bombing. We usually took off carrying 500-pound bombs and a full load of ammunition and went hunting for enemy shipping. When we saw enemy planes they were usually high and far away. On the few occasions when they came down to fight they made a few passes and then broke it off.

After the fall of Africa my squadron left the 57th Fighter Group and returned to our old 324th Group that we had left at Kabrit in Egypt three months before. Group headquarters were established at a new airfield, a dried-up lake bed on Cape Bon near Tunis. We moved from Qairouan to Cape Bon on June 20 and the next day began a new assignment.

For three weeks we escorted medium and heavy bombers over Sicily in the softening-up stage for the coming invasion. This was our worst and roughest assignment. On every mission we were hit by large formation's of ME-109's and Focke-Wulf 190's. Not a day passed without aerial combat and a few more planes shot down. The losses we suffered made a lasting impression on us and gave us more respect for the German Air Force. In addition, flak was always heavy and cost us more casualties.

We were outmatched by the Germans and we knew it. It wasn't a question of pilots; I think we had the edge. But our P-40's were no match for the higher-performing Nazi fighters, and every time we tangled they were sure to get some of our boys. We were begging for P-51 Mustangs, newer and faster airplanes, but they were needed in England for long-range bomber escort over Germany. So we used what we had and made the best of it.

Our D-day assignment was dawn patrol over the invasion beaches. Early on July 10 we took off in darkness and

Me-109

crossed the narrow straits, arriving over Sicily at sunrise. Below us our bombers were flooding inland against enemy strong points, the paratroopers in transports and gliders moving in behind them. Enemy fighter opposition over the beaches was light. Down on the ground the infantry began moving ashore despite high seas and enemy resistance. Behind them navy guns and rockets supported their assault as they scrambled to higher ground and dug in.

In the air we had the most trouble from our own troops. Friendly ack-ack began shooting with the first light of morning at every plane in the sky. I was shot at several times by our own antiaircraft batteries and another squadron lost one P-40. Losses were especially severe among our gliders and C-47's. We flew several more beach patrols over Sicily before friendly flak ceased to be a problem, but by the end of July the beachheads were secure and the invasion was well inland. Our mission accomplished, we were released from combat to regroup and replace our losses.

We spent three more months at Cape Bon, repairing battle-damaged planes, scrounging for new ones, and training fresh pilots. It was a waiting period, but after two campaigns in five months I found it welcome. In August I was promoted to captain. Soon afterward the Ninth Air Force in Africa disbanded and reformed in England and we transferred to the new Twelfth Air Force under General Spaatz.

The invasion of Italy was nearly two months old when we moved from Tunisia to a new airstrip in the vineyards on the slopes of Mt. Vesuvius. We found quarters in modern apartment houses near Naples and lived in high fashion. We doubled up two to a room, with private baths in each apartment, and indoor plumbing. Downstairs we set up a group mess, a bar, and gambling rooms. After living mostly in tents for the past year, even wartime Naples was a luxury. We rode to the airfield in jeeps and flew in clean uniforms. Upon returning from missions we entered the waiting jeeps and drove to downtown Naples for an evening of entertainment.

Missions in Italy were mostly strafing and dive bombing —the dirty work of fighters. Railroads and bridges were the usual targets at first. The front was up north a few miles above Naples and after a while we began flying support for the infantry against enemy gun positions. They were heavily defended and I was hit several times by flak.

Through November and December we kept up the pressure from the air while the foot soldiers slogged it out on the ground. In January I began leading the squadron against gun positions in front of the Fifth Army. In the mountainous country of southern Italy the German strong points were almost impregnable to ground assault. One of these strong points was the Benedictine abbey on Monte Cassino.

Twice on January 3rd and again on January 6 my squadron attacked gun positions in this area. On the morning of January 7 the briefing officer told us that our target was Monte Cassino. Our assignment was to destroy the abbey and other buildings on top of the mountain to force a German evacuation. I led the squadron out on the first strikes against the abbey.

The whole group of thirty-six planes flew two missions over Monte Cassino, attacking the target with guns and bombs. For the next two days it was under heavy bombardment from all types of aircraft and heavy ground fire from artillery. I still don't know if there were enemy troops in the abbey or its buildings, and I was too busy at the time leading my squadron to give it any thought. We were directed to accomplish a mission and we carried it out without any qualms.

The rest of January we continued to attack German gun positions along the southern front with 500- and 1,000-pound bombs. Occasionally isolated enemy fighters jumped us but we drove them off without serious losses. But air opposition was no measure of German resistance, for despite everything we threw at the enemy, the war remained deadlocked on the ground. In an effort to break the deadlock a beachhead was established at Anzio and we were called on to cover the landings.

My own part in the show was fairly brief. I was up three times over the beaches the first two days of the landing, trying to cover the infantry and keep the German dive bombers off their backs. This was pretty hard to do because the Jerries usually came in high and dove down through our formations to unload their bombs, then continued at high speed back to their bases.

Fw-190

We were hit several times by 109's and 190's, but they showed no desire to stay and fight, and would make their bomb runs and strafing passes and keep right on going. We had Spitfires flying patrol at higher altitudes and they were able to engage the Germans more successfully because of their greater speed. After the first day, German antiaircraft fire was heavy and gave us the most trouble.

Early in February, Bob Worley and I completed our combat tour and were ordered home for rest leave. While we awaited transportation I occupied myself for several days flying Army mail to the beachhead at Anzio.

This was a volunteer assignment, flying an Air Corps C-61 liaison plane from Fifth Army headquarters at Caserta near Naples. I offered to help because there weren't enough Army pilots to meet the need. I flew eight round trips to Anzio in five days, taking mail from home to the beach and returning with letters from our troops to be mailed at Caserta.

The distance is less than a hundred miles direct, but I took a roundabout route that covered closer to 150. From Caserta I flew out to sea to get beyond range of enemy shore batteries, then headed northwest toward Anzio, taking care to fire the colors of the day as I approached Allied shipping to prevent them from shooting at me.

I went in to the beach at low altitude, sometimes under shellfire, landing on a temporary airstrip near the water. They expected me, of course, and after taxiing to a halt, I jumped out of the little Fairchild monoplane with the engine still running. I laid the mail on the sand and yelled at them to bring the other mail over. They ran over and gave me several bags of letters to take back. I hurriedly threw these in the rear of the cockpit and climbed in immediately and took off.

After ninety-six combat missions the war in Italy ended for me. With mixed feelings I flew to Algeria and boarded a ship at Oran bound for Newport News. It was good being home at first, being with Avis and Mom and Dad, and seeing my friends and relatives in Fairmont. After sixteen months overseas I was glad to forget the war. I bought a secondhand car and the local police judge gave me back my driver's license, and after two weeks in Fairmont Avis and I drove to the Air Corps rest camp for combat returnees at Miami Beach.

It was here that the reaction set in. I felt hopelessly lost at Miami, partly because of the enforced idleness, but mostly because of the contrast to my life of action during the past year and a half. I was one of thousands of pilots at Miami, all combat veterans like myself, and somehow everything suddenly seemed a waste of time. After living under the tension of war for so long, being back in America was a sudden and shocking letdown.

Even my relationship with Avis was strained. This girl whom I had known all my adult life, and to whom I was married, suddenly seemed a stranger. After the newness wore off, we both felt ill at ease. We did not disagree violently about anything, but there was no close feeling of comradeship. It was not conducive to any high degree of happiness or stable conditions.

From Miami I was sent to a fighter training unit at Venice, Florida, where we found a place to live. Much to my disgust it was another P-40 outfit. Here I was put to work teaching combat tactics to second lieutenants on their way overseas as replacement pilots. I began flying again, however, and with my time occupied once more, life became bearable.

I checked out in every kind of airplane available to me— A-20's, P-47's, A-24's, A-25's, and one C-78. It was mostly curiosity—I wanted to see how they flew. I was stuck in the P-40 for instruction, but we enjoyed flying it in mock combat against other training units in our vicinity. We especially liked to jump the P-51 boys to see if we could outsmart them. The P-51 became an obsession with me; it was beautiful and wicked-looking, and after dogfighting with it a few times I fell in love with the plane.

But eventually even flying became dull and I longed to return to combat. While I knew my work was important, still I felt that I was not making my full contribution to the war effort. I felt that I was shirking my duty training second lieutenants, and I wanted to return to combat and try to shoot down more enemy planes. This feeling grew on me until I could stand it no longer, and at that point I told my squadron commander that I was fed up and wanted to go back overseas.

Although somewhat startled, he granted my request, and orders were cut for me to report to the overseas replacement depot at Tallahassee. To my disgust they put me down as a

P-47

replacement pilot for P-40's, an airplane which I had now flown several hundred hours. I balked at this. I told them I had enough of P-40's and dive bombing and strafing; I wanted to go overseas in P-51's and use my experience in aerial combat where it would do the most good. They turned me down, however, because I had never flown a P-51.

Immediately I asked for an opportunity to get some P-51 time. This apparently made sense to them, because they offered to see what could be done. The next day I was sent to a fighter training unit near St. Petersburg for three days of P-51 training. Feeling much better, I drove to Pinellis on special orders, checked out in the airplane, and flew it five times. Then I drove back to Tallahassee to await overseas transportation.

England was my first preference for a new combat assignment. They had P-51's and during the previous spring and summer the German Air Force had been very active. But it was October now, and it seemed to me that the air war in Europe had slowed down. From what I heard, the need for fighter pilots had decreased over there and I decided I could make a greater contribution in the Pacific war. I also thought I would find the air war in the China-Burma-India theater the more active at that juncture, so I requested assignment to the CBI.

I tried to explain to Avis my reasons for applying for a second tour of duty overseas: that I had to go, that with my experience I felt at a loss remaining in the States and had the feeling that I wasn't doing my duty, and that by returning to combat I believed I could help to do what needed to be done. I think she understood this to a considerable degree although she was still shocked and hurt by the fact that I wanted to go away so soon, and leave her to fly airplanes.

Even had it been possible, however, I do not think I would have changed my mind. After taking Avis home to Fairmont and visiting my parents, I flew to Miami to proceed overseas. As our C-54 transport taxied out and took off, I was conscious of conflicting emotions. I was relieved to be on my way at last and I felt that I was doing the right thing; but at the same time I felt that perhaps I was pushing my luck too hard. Watching out the window as the Florida coast line passed beneath us, I had a foreboding that I might not return.

I knew that I had had my share of luck in Africa and Italy; perhaps the odds against me had reached the point of diminishing returns. Shaking myself to thrust the idea from my mind, I turned back to my companions in the airplane and reached for a cigarette. But it was an effort to smile and talk. Apprehension akin to fear traveled with me, and despite all I could do it remained in my thoughts.

4

Prisoner

The staging area at Karachi was only a stop en route, a few days waiting for orders to continue on to China. I was one of hundreds of pilots in the combat replacement depot, but a personal visit to the commanding officer stating that I had previous combat time got quick results. Within forty-eight hours I was on board another transport plane headed east, and late in November I landed at the headquarters of the 14th Air Force in Kunming, China.

Kunming was a dirty, poor, war-weary city, far different from my conception of the mysterious East. I was assigned to quarters in miserable barracks at the American airfield on the edge of town, and went to bed that night depressed and wondering why I had come.

The next morning I walked across the field to the personnel office at 14th Air Force headquarters to report in and request assignment to an active combat unit. The personnel officer told me that no vacancies existed. Both the 23rd and 56th Fighter Groups, equipped with P-51 fighter planes, had their full complement of pilots and I would have to wait my turn. As the CBI theater was comparatively inactive at the end of 1944, with small combat losses, the available manpower exceeded requirements. Fuel and ammunition were limited because of the long supply routes, and since the bombers got first call, the fighter outfits were rationed. All the squadrons were overstaffed with replacement pilots and they had little opportunity to build up combat missions.

Sitting around my barracks that night, I received a visit

from Major Jim Dale, a squadron commander from the Fifth Fighter Group at Chihkiang. This was a Chinese-American Composite Wing, better known as CACW, composed of American pilots and officers in command assignments, with Chinese pilots and ground crew personnel. Chihkiang was farther east in Hunan Province, about 400 miles from the Japanese-occupied city of Hankow. Unlike the P-51 outfits at Kunming, Dale said the Fifth Fighter Group needed American flight leaders, and he invited me to apply for assignment. But when he told me it was a P-40 outfit I told him I was not interested. I explained that I had flown ninety-six missions in P-40's in the Mediterranean theater and did not want anything more to do with them. I said they were a nice airplane but would not shoot down anything but balloons, and I preferred to wait for assignment to P-51's.

Despite my refusal, Major Dale requested me for his outfit, and a day or two later orders were cut transferring me to Chihkiang. I protested vehemently to the personnel officer but he said my orders were signed by General Chennault, commanding general of the 14th Air Force, and could not be changed. With a long face and bitterness in my heart, I returned to my barracks and packed my flight bag, and with Jim Dale leading the way, flew a P-40 to Chihkiang.

It was a miserable mud village on top of a hill; the barracks were filthy and crowded. I was assigned to the 17th Fighter Squadron commanded by Major John L. Ramsay. He was a tall Texas lad well liked by everyone in his outfit, and we soon became good friends. As I got to know some of the boys and began flying once more, I accepted the fact that I was again stuck in P-40's and began having a good time.

We flew constantly against Japanese troops, supply centers, and lines of communication, ranging as far as Hankow 400 miles northeast and beyond. Most of the work was strafing and dive-bombing roads, rivers, bridges, and troop columns. On my first combat mission in China I strafed and destroyed five railroad tank cars. We also attacked Japanese shipping along the Yangtze River between Chihkiang and Hankow, attacking the little river boats and sampans with machine-guns and 500-pound bombs.

Much of the time I flew as wing man with the group commander, Colonel John ("Killer") Dunning, another Texan and a personal friend. Whenever he could get away from the paperwork involved in running four squadrons of P-40's and two B-25 and P-38 squadrons attached to the group, we went out flying. Usually the two of us went by ourselves, looking for trouble and most of the time finding it. He issued standing orders to the group never to bring back any bombs or ammunition. Scarce as they were, fuel was even scarcer, and we had instructions to empty our bomb racks and cartridge belts regardless of the target, rather than burn precious gasoline flying ammunition back to the base.

We were one of the last two fighter groups in China to fly P-40's. Early in February, 1945, they were replaced with P-51's, enough for three squadrons, including mine, and at long last I found myself flying combat in my dream airplane.

Shortly thereafter I was made acting squadron commander of the 29th Fighter Squadron, replacing another major returning to the States on rotation. This was a job I found much to my liking. Colonel Dunning gave each squadron its own territory of operations, with the assignment of patrolling the area and disrupting enemy communications. We were to keep

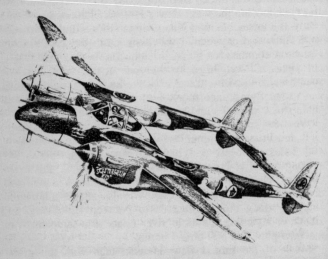

P-38 Lightning

all airfields free of enemy planes, knock out all railroad bridges, and attack supply lines and troop movements. This included both land and water routes using horse, truck, and boat.

In April I got a new squadron operations officer, Captain Nick Turner, who had lost a brother in combat and hated Japs. He was a real likable guy and very eager; we struck up a friendly relationship immediately and began flying together. Usually Nick and I would go out on reconnaissance sweeps early in the morning, knocking out bridges and shooting up Jap troop movements and supply columns.

Late in May, on a reconnaissance mission near Hankow, we spotted a large concentration of trucks and horses. We expended all our ammunition with good results, and to complete the job we returned to Chihkiang for the rest of the squadron. On the way back we flew down the Yangtze River, one on each bank, looking for Japanese boats tied up and camouflaged waiting for darkness, and marked their locations on our maps. We found several boats that looked like good targets and then returned to base and landed.

When we had refueled and the squadron was ready to go out, I told Nick to go ahead and lead the mission. I said that I had some administrative duties that required my attention and I would stay at the field and take care of them. Nick immediately rejoined, "What's the matter, Pete? No guts?" This was the kind of good-natured kidding I was used to, but nonetheless it irritated me a little. "I'll be flying when you're dead," I replied. Without further ado I picked up my helmet and parachute and walked out to my airplane, his remark still rankling.

A new boy was flying wing for me, a second lieutenant on his first combat mission, and I wanted to make sure he learned the proper method of combat. Nick was flying on my left. We briefed the other two flights to polish off the remaining trucks and horses in the Japanese supply column near Hankow, and with our two wing men we headed up the river to find the Japanese boats. I considered them a better target because I liked to blow their boilers with machine-gun bullets and set them on fire; to me it was more enjoyable shooting up boats than strafing trucks and trying to stampede horses.

We found the first two boats tied up on the river bank and sank them. Then we continued to the next boat 25 or 30 miles farther. This one was fairly large and looked like a good target for a strafing run. Calling on my wing man to stay close and follow me in, I came down from 3,000 feet in a high-speed pass and gave it two or three long bursts amidships.

I did not pop the boiler nor did I see any sign of smoke or fire. This annoyed me to a certain degree, and instead of pulling up as I should have done and setting up another high-speed pass, I racked the P-51 around on its wing tip in a low-level turn. I came back in on the deck, 10 or 15 feet off the water, at a fairly slow speed of 150 miles an hour. I began rudder-walking and firing at the same time to make sure I put the maximum amount of lead on the target, and as I did so I was hit by Japanese machine-gun fire.

One slug knocked a hole in the fire wall in front of the cockpit. Another shell hit the coolant tank of my liquid-cooled Allison engine. The boiling coolant streamed back into the cockpit, and as the scalding liquid struck my face and hands I cried out despite myself and jerked the canopy open.

If I had to bail out I wanted to be as far away as possible from the Japanese gun positions on the river bank. Half-blinded by the burning coolant, I pulled the nose of the airplane up sharply and headed across the river. The pain was acute. Over the far shore I could not stand it any longer and yelled over the radio that I was getting out.

In my pain and excitement I was confused. Pulling myself erect in the cockpit, I attempted to crawl over the left side. This was a mistake, because it exposed me to the blast of the prop wash that came back over the left side of the airplane. As I dragged myself over the side of the cockpit my parachute caught on the armor plating and I hung helplessly in the prop wash trying to free myself.

I beat on the side of the fuselage with both fists to no avail. I was still in pain and unable to see clearly. The P-51 was losing altitude rapidly, so I tried to get back in the cockpit and get out the other side. As I did so my parachute harness freed itself and I slid back against the tail of the airplane and then out into space.

Feeling myself free at last, I pulled the ripcord and my chute opened. Below me to the left the P-51 struck the ground and exploded with a loud "boom" like cannon fire. I landed in a rice paddy near the river, knee-deep in water and mud which broke my fall. I shucked my parachute, strapped on my jungle kit, and took my service revolver from its shoulder holster. Except for the burns on my face and hands and a pain in my ribs where I'd struck the plane, I was uninjured.

Nearby was a Chinese farmer working in the rice field, and I motioned to him to approach me. My first thought was to find friendly Chinese who would return me to friendly territory. I knew that I was deep inside the Japanese lines and had no chance of escaping without Chinese help. Taking my Chinese-English dictionary from the escape kit strapped around my waist, I tried to ask the farmer my location. All our conversation produced was some primitive sign language that I took to mean a village was in vicinity. Waving good-by to Nick Turner and my wing man, who hovered anxiously overhead, I began walking in that direction.

I had a feeling of apprehension approaching the little village, not knowing whether it concealed Japanese troops, and fully aware that I would probably be killed if taken prisoner. As I entered the outskirts a crowd of Chinese civilians gathered about me. One or two spoke pidgin-English. I told them who I was and explained my desire to return to American lines, and asked if there were any guerrillas in the vicinity who could help me. After I finished talking the group began animatedly discussing me in Chinese. I was unable to understand them, but judging from their faces I thought they were arguing among themselves and I feared that some of them wanted to turn me over to the Japs.

After this had gone on several minutes, I decided that I was getting nowhere and began to walk away. At this they called me back and argued several minutes longer. Then one of them detached himself from the group and motioned me to follow him. I was tired from having flown twice that day and still nervous and upset from my bailout, but I followed him. The sun was already low in the west. There was no indication on his part where we were going, but I had no alternative except to wander alone and hope to find guerrilla troops; so I gave him the benefit of the doubt and we started off.

We walked fairly steadily four or five hours south along the river. Darkness had fallen and there was no one on the road but ourselves. About midnight we came to another village and went to a house where we were met by a Chinese man and woman. I was given a little bowl of rice, which I ate hungrily, and then I was made to understand that I could lie down on a straw covering on the floor and rest.

Although I was exhausted by this time, I had not fallen asleep before I was roused by the sound of voices, and looking up I saw three Chinese soldiers in uniform. They motioned to me to follow them and hurried off. It seemed odd to me that guerrilla troops should be wearing Chinese army uniforms so deep inside the Japanese lines, but they made no attempt to disarm me, so I assumed they were friendly and stumbled along behind them in the darkness.

Half an hour later I saw lights ahead and then we passed through sentry lines and I found myself in a troop compound filled with several hundred Chinese in uniform. The night was clear and the moon was full, and I could see the river in the distance. My guides took me to a one-room shack lighted by an oil lamp and furnished with a desk and several chairs. Here I was greeted by a young officer who spoke broken English, and he identified himself as Captain Ching, the commanding officer.

He ordered a soldier to bring me rice and water, which I ate and drank. Then I told him I wanted help. I said that the American authorities would pay him $20,000 for my safe return and asked him to take me to the nearest friendly troops; after much discussion he agreed and then I left to get some sleep.

In the morning, I was wakened early, shaved from head to toe, and dressed in a Chinese uniform. Then I was taken outside and told to mount a Chinese horse. Captain Ching was waiting for me, together with two lieutenants and a dozen soldiers. He asked me to give him my gun and wedding ring and wrist watch. I objected, but he explained that we might be observed by hostile troops who would see through my disguise. For a moment I wondered why a Chinese disguise was safer than an American uniform in hostile territory; but I was in no position to argue with him so I acceded to his request and we started off.

Upon leaving the compound our little party headed north, which was the wrong direction, as the American lines lay south of us. After riding for an hour with no change in the way we were going, I called on the Chinese to stop and told Captain Ching to turn south. He explained there were Japanese forces in that direction and that we would have to circle around them. This made sense to me so I told him to proceed.

We continued northward all day, crossing many small streams and skirting the shores of lakes. Several times we used sampans and swam the horses. Now and then we passed other Chinese troops and encountered civilians on farms and in the occasional small villages. By evening I was thoroughly alarmed. I knew from my location that we must be very near the large city of Hankow, which was held by the Japanese. At any moment I expected to encounter them on the highway.

Around dusk we met a motor convoy of Chinese troops and Captain Ching stopped to talk to the commander. After some discussion I was told to get in one of the trucks and lie down. Several soldiers got in beside me and sat between me and the entrance. Then the truck started up and we drove slowly into Hankow.

As we jolted through the Japanese outposts on the edge of the city, the uniforms of Japanese soldiers were visible from time to time as I looked through the canvas covering. Even had escape been possible, it was too late now. About midnight we drove into a Chinese troop compound in the center of the city and I got out of the truck. Captain Ching appeared and took me into one of the barracks to a room with a bed. He indicated that I should rest and said he would return in the morning. No sooner had my head touched the pillow than I fell fast asleep.

It was daylight when I was awakened by a large and hostile-looking Japanese officer prodding me vigorously with the tip of a large and ugly-looking sword. Two impassive Japanese soldiers handcuffed me and tied my ankles with rope hobbles to prevent my running. Then I was pushed roughly outside and the officer motioned me to follow him, with the soldiers carrying loaded rifles bringing up the rear.

We crossed the river on a footbridge, hostile and angry glances from several spectators following me as I passed through the crowd. At the headquarters building on the far side of the Yangtze I was thrown into a basement cell. The only outside opening was a small barred window at sidewalk level on the street. My handcuffs and hobbles were removed but the outside corridor was patrolled by armed guards. Thus the day passed without food or water. In the evening I was given a pot of rice to eat and something to drink. That night I was attacked by swarms of mosquitoes. My only covering was two blankets, which I used to make a pallet on the floor. The cell was stifling hot, but the mosquitoes were even worse, and finally I wrapped myself completely in one of the dirty wool blankets, leaving just a small hole over my face to breathe through. In this fashion I spent a miserable, agonizing night of fitful slumber, not knowing what new hardships day might bring.

In the morning I was given a little more rice and water and then was led upstairs for my first interrogation. The intelligence officer, a captain, spoke excellent English; he told me he had grown up in the United States and had been graduated from Columbia University in New York. It was such a relief to speak English again that I relaxed despite myself. The lieutenant with him was hostile and belligerent toward me; he spoke enough English to tell me how many battles he had fought and the number of Americans he had slain in hand-to-hand combat, and I decided that he was trying to frighten me.

They were very pleasant at first. The captain asked me if I needed anything, and as I was hungry and thirsty I said so. Fine, he replied, we want to ask you a few questions first, and then you can eat all you wish.

With that he pushed a mimeographed piece of paper across the table where we sat and handed me a pencil. Glancing through it hurriedly, I saw detailed questions regarding my squadron and group, all of which I was unwilling to answer because of the nature of the information. Looking up, I explained I was not permitted to answer such questions; and filling in my name, rank, and serial number, I shoved the blank questionnaire back across the table.

Seeing that I was adamant, they summoned the guard and ordered me removed. I was led back down three flights of stairs to my basement dungeon and the door was locked behind me. Thus the day passed. At noon and in the evening I was given only a bowl of rice to eat, and my hunger increased. The night was a repetition of the heat and mosquitoes of the previous evening. In the morning I was interrogated again with the same results.

By this time I was demoralized by hunger and thirst. Although I had resolved to resist their questions, I began to feel that in my weakened and frightened condition I might not succeed.

We went through the same rigmarole of name, rank, and serial number and as time passed my tormentors became increasingly hostile. At the end of an hour I was taken back to my cell.

The third morning I was again taken to the interrogation room and questioned and again I shook my head when they asked me for information. Seeing that I was resolved not to talk, the captain gave a command in Japanese and the lieutenant got up and opened the door. Outside for the first time I saw a small courtyard, and in the middle of the yard was a block of wood. Two guards came in and pulled me to my feet and motioned me outside. The captain followed me out and told me I was to be executed. A large audience of officers had gathered in the yard for the occasion.

The block of wood, about two feet high, was covered by a rusty red substance that I took to be human blood. I was handcuffed and forced to my knees beside it. A soldier brought out a wicker basket which he placed beside the block, apparently where my head was to fall after it was lopped from my torso. The captain again asked me if I was ready to talk, and when I still replied in the negative, he gave the command to proceed with the execution.

The lieutenant had been standing nearby, swinging his heavy sword through the air and striking it against various objects lying about the yard to test its temper. I thought he might be bluffing but of course I was in no position to gamble. He now told me to place my head on the chopping block, which I did. He took a position beside me, like a batter ready to hit a baseball, and touched the blade of his sword on the back of my neck. The feel of the cold steel went through me like an electric shock.

Watching him from the corner of my eye, I saw him raise the sword experimentally a few times and then take a full backward swing. As he did so I straightened up and told him to stop. Trying to appear calm and cool, I turned to the captain and told him in English that perhaps there was something I could tell him after all.

This didn't please him; he had apparently called in several high-ranking officers to witness the ceremony and he felt they would be disappointed.

They conferred briefly in Japanese and then he told me to get up and return to the interrogation room. Hiding my feeling of great relief, I knew that now I had the upper hand and was in a position to bargain with him. So I told him pointblank as soon as we sat down at the table that there were definite limits on what I could say.

I would not answer any questions regarding the identity and location of my unit or any of its personnel. I would refuse to tell him where I was stationed or anything about the composition and strength of my outfit. However, I might be able to answer questions about the airplane which we operated, and since this seemed agreeable to him, we proceeded to talk about the P-51.

We had been told by our intelligence people that we could discuss the planes we flew if necessary to save ourselves from physical harm. The enemy had by this late date captured enough American planes to have a pretty good idea of their performance anyway. But the Japanese were not mechanically-minded and we knew they were never certain that the information they obtained was accurate; for this reason, they always respected and accepted any performance data that we gave them.

I answered questions about the speed, range, armament, and bomb load of the P-51, adding 50 or 100 per cent to the true figures to be sure the information would not be useful. I doubled the range and bomb load, increased the cruising speed from 250 to 325 miles an hour and said the plane had eight .50-caliber machine guns. They wrote all this down and appeared to be satisfied. I was returned to my cell and the next morning went back upstairs for another interrogation. They repeated the questions from the previous day, apparently to check up on me, and I carefully gave the same answers. I was very weak by now from hunger and lack of sleep but tried to appear composed and relaxed. Again they asked me to identify my unit and its location and again I refused. I spent the remainder of the day in my prison cell, and the next morning was moved to a new jail.

Treatment there was somewhat better. The building was cooler; the mosquitoes had mysteriously vanished. Food had also improved. Interrogation continued but was halfhearted, as if they did not really expect me to answer their questions now. After two weeks of this I was placed on a train with two Japanese guards, traveling only by night because of possible attacks by American planes in the daylight hours, and after a week of travel in darkness, we reached the Chinese city of Nanking.

I was weak from malnutrition and any physical exertion left me trembling and short of breath. But my burns had healed and the bruises received in bailing out had disappeared. My clothes were dirty and lice-infested. I still wore the Chinese uniform given me when I was captured and had a loose growth of beard. Otherwise I took occasional sponge baths and kept myself reasonably clean.

In Nanking there was another week of interrogations by Army, Navy, and Air Force officers but I told them nothing new about the American forces. My jail was another one-room cell with two blankets to sleep on. From Nanking I was moved again by train with Japanese guards, a long journey with daylight stops. Early in July we reached the northern city of Peiping.

Back home in Fairmont, Avis had been told in a War Department telegram on June 14 that I was missing in action after bailing out when flak hit my plane, but she did not know if I was dead or alive. But she believed—perhaps because it was the only thing she would admit to herself—that I was still all right. Even when she received a letter from General Chennault stating that "lack of news leaves little basis for optimism . . . in the light of our experience in this area," she did not give up hope. On Father's Day she bought a necktie for my dad, knowing I would want to remember him. It was all she could do for me, but it helped.

I again went through the familiar routine of jail and interrogation in Peiping, but this time it was a mere formality. Here for the first time I found other American prisoners, two pilots like myself. At the end of July we were moved from the jail in the city to Fengtai prison camp in abandoned warehouses on the edge of Peiping. Here we were confined with 300 civilians of many nationalities who had been held prisoner since they were captured in the fall of Shanghai in 1942. Most were from the international settlement in that city and had been confined there until allied air raids forced their removal farther north. I was one of only three military prisoners at Fengtai and the ranking officer.

The camp commandant was a Japanese colonel but we had Formosan guards. They were friendly to the civilian prisoners and some of them had struck up acquaintances. It was from them that we learned early in August that the Japanese had surrendered and hostilities had ended. Upon hearing this wonderful news, as ranking officer I requested an audience with the camp commandant, and through an interpreter asked him if the war was over.

He confirmed the surrender news but said he had not yet received official confirmation and in the meantime he had no orders to release us. I immediately demanded that he turn the camp over to me and instruct his troops to obey my orders. This he declined to do. He explained that there was bad feeling between the civilian internees and their captors and he was afraid that I would be unable to control either side. But he gave us the freedom of the camp and with this concession I returned to my quarters.

The next day I received word that Commander Wade Cunningham and other survivors of the American naval garrison at Wake Island were confined in a Peiping prison. I returned immediately to the commandant's office and demanded that these men be released and placed under my authority. A day or two later Commander Cunningham and five companions were brought to Fengtai. The commander was a very sick man, suffering badly from malnutrition. He was able to talk with me for only short periods of time before he became tired and had to rest. He told me that they had tried several times to escape and the last time were sentenced to life imprisonment. I realized that, by comparison, I had been very lucky as a prisoner.

On August 15 I was summoned to the commandant's office and there was greeted by an American Army major and three enlisted men from a prisoner-of-war team. They had parachuted into Peiping that morning to contact prisoners and internees in the area and to arrange for their removal to friendly hands. That evening I made my first trip outside the prison camp in freedom to visit the major at his Peiping hotel. Here I told him more about Fengtai and its inmates and he asked me to take charge of evacuating them. The next day the Japanese authorities in the city sent trucks and moving vans to Fengtai and transported all of us to the Wagons-Lits Hotel.

There were rumors that the remaining Doolittle raiders were also held in Peiping, those who had bombed Tokyo early in the war and failed to return. The second day in the hotel I was called from my office by a Japanese guard I had stationed at the entrance and found a covered truck at the curb guarded by a Japanese soldier. Upon my arrival he opened the truck and six Americans crept out. They were in very bad physical condition. Most were suffering from malnutrition and one was a litter case. They consisted of a pilot, a copilot, a navigator, a radio operator and two gunners—the Doolittle boys who were still alive.

I identified myself and told them they were free men. I said the Japanese had surrendered and the war was over. For a moment they refused to believe me, then they broke into tears of joy and hugged and kissed me. Their heads had been freshly shaved the day before and they'd thought they were on the way to their executions.

On August 20 the American military personnel at Peiping, including the survivors of the Wake Island defenders and the Doolittle raiders, were placed aboard a B-24 bomber at the Japanese airfield on the outskirts of the city and flown out to Kunming. I watched Peiping disappear in the distance with a deep feeling of relief and thankfulness I had come through the past three months of imprisonment unscathed and I was very glad to be alive; best of all, the shooting and killing were finally over.

From Kunming I was flown west to India, Africa, and on to America, landing at LaGuardia Field in New York City on September 4. But even before I came home, Avis received a telegram from the War Department, telling her that I was alive. When I telephoned her from the airport, she knew that I was safe and was waiting for my call.

We met at last in Washington, both of us a little shy and nervous, but both very grateful and glad now that the miracle had come true. This time being home was wonderful and rewarding. After what I had seen and experienced during the past months, I realized how much I had to be thankful for. We made no plans right away, but we both took it for granted that I would go on flying. Airplanes and the Air Force now were too deeply a part of our lives to start over. But what I would fly, and where, we were content to decide in the bright and limitless future.

5

Test Pilot

From home leave in Fairmont I was sent to the Army Air Corps replacement center at Greensboro, North Carolina, early in November, 1945, to await reassignment. Avis was expecting her first baby. We got a room at the O. Henry Hotel and I reported in at the base headquarters on the edge of town. With the war over, there was nothing to do, and after checking at the personnel office each morning to see if my orders had come through, I went back to the hotel for the rest of the day. I was one of thousands of officers and enlisted men in Greensboro en route some place; the only difference was that they were going home.

Like a few others, I wanted to stay in the Army. I liked the service and I wanted to keep on flying; what's more, I believed that aviation would grow. What my part in it would be, I was not certain at the moment; I knew the Air Corps would have to keep some of its planes, and perhaps I could go back to a fighter squadron. But I made no plans to be a civilian again, even tentatively; a military life was my only possible future.

From Greensboro Avis and I went to Craig Field, Alabama, a wartime air base now pressed into service as a separation center for flying personnel. Like Greensboro, it was jammed with soldiers. Housing was hard to find. We rented a furnished room in Selma, the nearest town, and ate in restaurants. To keep me busy, I was assigned to a refresher course at the air base, flying AT-6 trainers. In this way I occupied myself for one or two hours each morning; the rest of the day I spent with Avis in Selma.

We had Christmas leave in Fairmont and then I returned alone to Alabama. Living conditions were poor and Avis was sick a lot, so she decided to remain at home. With time on my hands, I took the opportunity to visit Eglin Field, Florida, in January, job-hunting. Eglin was being held as a postwar test base and I thought they might need a pilot. They didn't have a job at the moment, but were glad to put me on the waiting list. On the return trip I applied for an assignment at Bolling Field near Washington. Then I drove back to Selma.

January passed in depression and confusion. Every morning I went to the personnel office, hoping my number had come up. At least my records were in good shape; I had seen to that. I had insisted that my flying experience be spelled out in detail, including my qualification in nine different types of aircraft and my two years of engineering training in college. I knew that experience and education would weigh heavily in any future assignment.

My foresight bore fruit early in February when a selection team arrived from Air Materiel Command headquarters at Wright Field, Ohio, to look over the available pilots. Out of 800 flying officers awaiting reassignment at Craig Field, I was one of four chosen to report to Dayton. Our new assignment was to the fighter section of the flight test division at Wright Field, and the job was my dream come true—test pilot.

Of course I remembered Wright Field from prewar days; it was here that I had first applied for aviation cadet training in 1939. But like so many other things, the war had changed it too, and now instead of wooden hangars and grass runways I saw a much bigger air base with concrete strips and new permanent buildings.

On arrival my first official act was reporting in to my new commanding officer, Colonel Albert Boyd, chief of the flight test division. He was out of town on a cross-country flight, and in his absence his secretary suggested that we check in at the fighter section; we would be notified when to report back. Chief of the fighter section was Colonel Francis Gabreski, America's all-time fighter ace with 31 kills in the European theater. He was away too, however, and in his absence we reported to his assistant, Major Gus Lundquist.

He immediately told us that we were considered surplus. The fighter test section already had ten qualified pilots, more than enough to handle the test program on the few planes available. The war was over and new planes were not being built; the jet F-80 Shooting Star was the only fighter plane still in production. As a result, we would not be permitted to do test flying; if any planes became available, we could fly them when they were not being used; otherwise we would have to wait until other assignments were found for us.

At this kind of reception I got sore. I hadn't come all the way to Wright Field to be brushed off in this manner, and I made my mind up that I would stay if it was humanly possible. I wanted to do test flying and I was determined to demonstrate that I was qualified.

A week went by before Colonel Boyd called for us. As the ranking officer of our foursome, I entered his office first, and took an immediate liking to this stern, taciturn soldier. He was all business, a tall slender man with sandy hair, a lean face, and cool, searching eyes that seemed to look right through me. I looked back in a gaze equally searching, trying not to show my feelings, but ready to fight for what I wanted.

Remaining seated while we stood at attention, he proceeded to lecture us on what he appeared to think was our unforgiveable sin of coming to Dayton in the first place. He stated that he had not chosen us to be test pilots, that he preferred to select his own pilots, and as he did not know anything about our qualifications, we were considered surplus and probably would be transferred. In the meantime, we were to take orders from either Major Lundquist or his assistant, Captain Kenneth Chilstrom; and turning to me at this point, he said that I would consider Chilstrom my ranking officer, even though he was a captain and I was a major. I felt this was a little too much and that Colonel Boyd was being nastier than was necessary. However, I said nothing, and when he had finished we saluted and left his office.

My determination was still strong within me, however, and when I reached the waiting room I told his secretary I wanted to see him again. He looked up surprised and obviously displeased when I reappeared, but he put down the papers he was reading and leaned back in his chair to listen.

I told him I was very eager and highly desirous of remaining at Wright Field, and would he please keep this in mind? Prior to making any reassignment, if he could just give me a chance to show my stuff, I felt that I could do a good job for him, because I wanted to stay and was looking forward to this assignment.

He replied that he would look at our records carefully and we would be observed at all times. He said there was a slight chance we could be retained in the flight test division, but it was unlikely, and he thought we would all be transferred in the near future. With that he concluded our short interview and I saluted again and left.

Before a month passed the other three officers who came to Wright Field with me received new assignments elsewhere on the base. However, I continued in flight test on a day-to-day basis, flying anything I could at every opportunity, but never knowing when the ax would fall. I flew many times in airplanes I was already checked out in, wartime P-47's and P-51's, and also in the twin-engined P-38. This was no endorsement, however; the other pilots didn't particularly want to fly it, and it was just another job they could slop off on me. However, I welcomed the chance to show my flying ability, regardless of the airplane.

During these weeks I became good friends with Major Dick Johnson, one of the permanent pilots in the fighter section. We flew a lot together and when I told him how much I wanted to stay, he was interested and sympathetic. Dick was fairly close to Major Lundquist and Captain Chilstrom, and I feel that he was instrumental in their decision; when it came to a showdown on whether I was to be retained, he spoke up on my behalf.

The first indication that I might be accepted came early in May when Colonel William Councill, assistant chief of the flight test division, called me to his office to tell me that Bolling Field at Washington had requested me for duty as a statistical control officer. Did I wish to accept? I told him I would much prefer to remain at Wright Field and what were my chances? He said they were 50-50. If they were that good, I said, I would take the chance, and would he please turn down the request?

Unknown to me, another request came through from Eglin Field about the same time; Colonel Councill turned this down without informing me, which I realize now was a sure sign they were interested in keeping me at Wright Field. The first definite assurance I had was my assignment late in May to test pilot school. From this day on, I knew I had it made, and it was now entirely up to me whether I could cut the mustard and achieve my ambition to become a test pilot.

In the newly-organized school, with a handful of students, I would be taught how to test new planes for performance, stability, and control. If I demonstrated a reasonable ability in this work, there was no reason why I could not remain indefinitely in the job I wanted.

I soon found that testing an airplane required a lot more than just flying it. In the performance course we flew many hours at all speeds, altitudes, and power settings, keeping careful records of the results for future use in preparing a pilot's handbook. We shot many take-offs and landings. We learned how to read the special instruments installed in test planes to record flight information, and how to reduce these data afterward for the information of other pilots and engineers.

Although aircraft manufacturers had always tested their own planes, military testing was comparatively new. It began as an attempt to standardize performance data on all planes flown by the Air Force. Each manufacturer used his own test methods, and sometimes he would even take the optimistic side and report that performance was a little better than the facts warranted. He might say his airplane would go to 40,000 feet and fly 500 miles an hour, when actually it would only go to 35,000 feet and 450 miles an hour. It was our job to test the airplane for the Air Force and come up with the actual performance figures.

With the new jet F-80 in production and the F-84 on the way, the airplane was reaching new speeds in which faulty design characteristics were becoming critical. For this reason a course in stability testing was added to the curriculum at the pilot school in 1946, looking toward the time when it would become a standard test for all new fighter planes built for the Air Force. At the same time we decided to run control tests. They tie in together. You may have a stable airplane, but if the controls are too light or too heavy, the airplane cannot be maneuvered properly. Or it may be difficult to take off or land, which would make it hazardous to fly and increase the accident rate.

Aircraft have always had stability and control problems, but World War II airplanes such as the P-40 and P-51 did not reach speeds where it made too much difference. The P-40, for example, had a tendency to turn left on take-off, and the pilot had to use extra right rudder to keep it on the runway. This would not be considered acceptable today and the manufacturer would have to correct it. The B-25 bomber had a stability problem when flying at the aft center of gravity limit; if it were designed today we would ask the manufacturer to make it more stable.

Each airplane is built for a specific mission—the fighter plane is a gun platform, the bomber is a bomb platform. The more stable these platforms are, the easier it is to hit your target. If you have a gun platform that is yawing and bouncing around the sky, it is much more difficult to aim your guns. And if the bomber is moving around the sky and not going in the direction you want it to go, again you have an unstable platform.

As aircraft speeds increase, the manufacturer finds that stability and control problems grow correspondingly. He can build an airplane that takes off and lands at low speed, but it will be harder to control at high speeds because of the design of the control surfaces. So he must choose the design best suited to the speed regime where the plane will do most of its flying.

This is a Hobson's choice that bedevils every aircraft designer. In the F-84 jet fighter, for example, we found control was good around 350 miles an hour, which was fine for acrobatic flying in air shows, but not much help in combat missions at 600 miles an hour. Aileron and elevator effectiveness decreased both above and below this speed region. As a result, the manufacturer had to redesign these controls to be effective at all speeds.

It was not long before the flying skills and standards taught at test pilot school began to pay off in the improved performance and handling characteristics of new aircraft. At the same time the Air Force opened its school to test pilots of manufacturers, as well as the Navy and friendly foreign countries. This made it possible to standardize testing methods and reports from the first flights of prototype airplanes. Since then many Air Force pilots have left the service to test planes for manufacturers, further standardizing aircraft testing.

In the spring of 1946 I was checked out and authorized to fly in my first jet-powered airplane, the Bell P-59. The first airplane in America to fly on jet engines four years earlier, it was obsolete by now. It handled well but performance was disappointing, as it was underpowered and was more or less just a powered glider. I remember it today chiefly as my first experience with an airplane made by Bell Aircraft Corporation, which I later became identified with so closely.

What I noticed most at the time was the lack of noise and vibration common to piston-engined planes. I had a feeling of sailing through the air instead of rowing. On the other hand, acceleration was noticeably less, which increased the take-off run; and on landing the airplane decelerated more slowly because there was no propeller to act as an airbrake. In flight, of course, this was an advantage; it was not necessary to keep full power to maintain air speed, as even with reduced power the speed of the streamlined jet did not bleed off as rapidly as that of the propeller-driven plane.

Early in June I got my first ride in a newer jet, the Lockheed F-80. This was a single-engined fighter designed and built for jet power from the start. For several weeks I had watched other pilots fly it and talked to them about its performance; I had even gotten in the cockpit and started the engine. Because of my high degree of interest, when the time came to fly it I knew it better than most new planes.

Captain Martin L. Smith, who later was killed in an F-80 at Wright Field, checked me out. We went over the cockpit thoroughly and he assured himself that I knew the airplane. I started the engine and he told me to go ahead and take off. The mechanic took away the ladder and I closed and secured the plexiglas canopy. Then I called the tower on the radio and on receiving clearance taxied out and took off.

Although I had been thoroughly briefed on the F-80's improved characteristics, I was still not prepared for this new kind of performance. As it left the ground I tucked the wheels up in the wings and leveled off to gain climb speed and the fast little jet accelerated almost automatically. Less than a minute had elapsed before the airspeed indicator on the instrument panel read over 450 miles an hour. This was especially impressive to me because it was one of the few times I had flown this fast in any airplane, especially in level flight.

I pulled the nose up slightly to climb to higher altitude and set my course on a northerly heading. Completely lost in a new sensation of easy, effortless speed, after climbing for a short time I came out of my daze and looked around. The landscape below was unfamiliar, but I realized from my instruments that Wright Field was already 150 miles away. I turned back grudgingly, reluctant to end this new experience of free, untrammeled flight. With the field in sight again, I stalled the airplane and felt it out gently. Then I did some acrobatics and dive tests. It was highly responsive and handled beautifully. This was a new kind of flying such as I had never believed possible. More than an hour later, my fuel almost gone, I came in and landed, beside myself with the thrill of my first F-80 jet.

I also realized this was just a beginning and that new jets under construction would offer even higher speed and performance. In the F-80 we had just begun to attain the speed potential inherent in the jet engine. For this reason, I knew this was only a taste of things to come. I also realized it was the opening of a whole new era in aviation. Jets were the planes of the future and I was on the ground floor in their development and operation. With my early interest in speed still part of me, I looked forward to new thrills yet to come.

Upon graduation from test pilot school I was accepted for permanent duty in the flight test division, assigned to the fighter section under Major Lundquist. He had replaced Colonel Gabreski, who left the service for a job in private industry. Major Lundquist also left shortly to attend a university and was replaced by Kenneth Chilstrom, now a major. He in turn was succeeded shortly by Colonel Pat Fleming, a former Navy Pilot, with Dick Johnson as assistant chief.

I flew and tested all the airplanes of that day, both fighters and bombers. Colonel Boyd gave me the chance I wanted and I took every opportunity to gain experience. I flew at the drop of a hat, on weekends including Sundays. When I was in the vicinity, sometimes I flew over my home in Fairmont and buzzed the house or dropped notes to my parents from the plane. I flew in air shows and cross-country flights, piloting both prop jobs and jets. As I was away so much, inevitably our home life suffered. Avis was a flying widow for many long months, but she did not complain unduly. After the anxiety and uncertainty of the previous winter, she was glad to see me happy in my work, and even encouraged me to do more flying.

During my first months at Wright Field we had a satellite base at Muroc, California, to run accelerated service tests on the jet F-80. Among our pilots stationed at Muroc to conduct these tests were Major Dick Bong and Lieutenant Charles Yeager. Dick was a fighter ace in the Pacific during the war and later was killed in an F-80 accident. I met Chuck when he returned to Wright Field for several months and we flew many air shows together. Like myself, he is a native of West Virginia. Chuck was a small, quiet individual in those days, but had ability and courage to spare. Early in 1947 he was assigned to test the new Bell X-1 rocket plane and went back to Muroc. Later I followed him out there and we resumed our friendship.

About a year after I checked out in jets I began flying a new jet fighter plane, the Republic F-84 Thunderjet. This was a straight-wing monoplane with an axial-flow engine, in contrast to the centrifugal-flow type used in the F-80. Performance of the two planes was similar, although the F-84 was harder to fly. It was a heavier plane, giving it higher wing loading, and this limited its maneuverability a little more. As a result, I found it harder to do acrobatics and to put on an air show with this airplane, in comparison with the earlier jet.

I was the first military test pilot to fly stability and control tests on a new fighter plane, using the new B model of the F-84. At this time the jet was going into service with tactical units, and reports of trouble started coming back from the field. Several planes lost their wings in high-speed maneuvers and the pilots bailed out or were killed. We instrumented one of the new B airplanes and I took it up to find out why the wings were coming off.

I climbed to altitude to give me time to bail out if I got into trouble, then made several dive tests close to maximum speed to measure the stick forces on pullout. In these tests I was pulling up to five and six G's. After several flights I noted that the 84 was suffering a stick reversal; under certain conditions the stick would continue to come on back in my lap and the G forces would continue rising. It appeared from this evidence that some airplanes had been overstressed sufficiently to break off their wings.

We held several meetings with engineers from Republic Aviation Corporation and other aircraft manufacturers to discuss the problem. It was a serious one, as the F-84 was our newest jet. Out of these meetings came a decision by Republic to put a stronger wing on the F-84, redesign the control system, and modify the tail. When these changes were made the problem was licked.

Despite my training in test pilot school and my growing proficiency in many different planes, I still felt handicapped by my lack of academic training. I lacked a basic understanding of aerodynamics, which I realized would hold me back in flight testing. For the first time I was aware that the old-time test pilot was obsolete. The prewar aviators who flew by the seat of their pants and dove an airplane to its terminal velocity in an effort to destroy it were as out of date as the wood-and-canvas airplanes they flew.

With aircraft speeds increasing yearly, the postwar test pilot had to be a flying scientist. He would have to anticipate new problems and explain them when they showed up. I knew that airplanes were being designed and built with swept-back wings, and I had to find out why. I also knew they would have thinner wings and power-boosted controls to maneuver them at high speeds. If I expected to keep pace with aviation progress I needed to know more and understand better. As a result I spent many hours educating myself.

I talked with aircraft engineers and engineering pilots. I visited aircraft laboratories at Wright Field and read books on the new theories of aerodynamics. I have continued to do this throughout my career in flight testing. After a while I was able to understand the physical laws governing aircraft behavior at high speeds and to perform adequately when called upon to find a solution for a specific problem. I was usually able to understand what was occurring and to explain it later to the engineers. In this way I gradually acquired the skill and competence needed for flight testing in the new jet age. The early years at Wright Field were a constant but successful struggle to prove myself.

It was during these years, in the second half of the 1940's, that much of aviation's new high-speed flight equipment was designed and built. As test center for the Air Force, which would operate the new planes of the post-war era, Wright Field and the flight test division tested the new equipment and participated in its development. We as pilots conducted the tests, and out of our experience and recommendations, aircraft designers and manufacturers built better planes and weapons systems.

Working with our aeromedical laboratory, we flew many tests on standardized instrument panels and cockpits. Faster flight was sharply reducing the pilot's own reaction time, and with the advent of the jet airplane he needed to find his controls and see his instruments in a hurry. This served to emphasize the need to standardize the cockpit, with controls and instruments in the same place in all planes so the pilot could find them automatically.

After tests to find the best location, we recommended cockpit installations—how the controls should be shaped and where they should be put. Today we have finally realized a fairly standard cockpit. The presentation may differ slightly because of the differences in aircraft, but the throttle is always on the left, for instance, as are the landing gear and flap handles. As a result, it isn't too much of a problem for a pilot to go from one airplane to another.

The higher speeds and altitudes that could be reached with jet aircraft raised the immediate problem of pilot protection. How would we keep him warm at high altitudes, supplied with oxygen, and protected against atmospheric pressure? Most of my early jet flying was done without pressurization. I spent many a cold, miserable hour at 40,000 feet without pressure or cockpit heating, even having my feet frostbitten on one flight because I was unable to keep warm.

As a result of many tests and hardships, our third jet fighter plane, the F-86, had twice the cockpit pressurization of earlier jets, and better air conditioning. This meant that the pilot was twice as comfortable when flying at great heights. With a cockpit pressure of 20,000 feet at 40,000 feet altitude, for example, he found flying much easier because he was not forced to undergo pressure breathing with oxygen.

We were experimenting with different types of oxygen masks and pressure systems. We were used to the old type of pressure demand where we increased pressure manually as the plane went higher. After three or four flights a day with this system, I felt as if I had put in twenty hours on the road. But with the newer systems the oxygen pressure would increase automatically, which made it much easier on the pilot and conserved his energies for other duties.

The old-type oxygen masks were uncomfortable, as they had to be airtight to prevent leaks and required an extremely close fit. Equally unsatisfactory were the old cloth-and-leather helmets. In jet airplanes at high speeds, buffeting was a constant hazard, and the wartime helmets no longer protected the pilot if his head struck the cockpit or canopy. Both problems were met and overcome in the new crash helmets developed at Wright Field for jet and rocket planes. These rigid plastic helmets are standard equipment today for all jet pilots.

At the same time we ran development tests on an improved "G" suit. This is another essential piece of equipment in high-speed flight to protect the pilot in violent turns and maneuvers. Without a G suit to hold him together, he can black out or red out under positive or negative acceleration. We rode many times on the centrifuge, a device that tested our resistance to G's, or the pull of gravity. After finding our G-tolerance, the point at which we lost consciousness, we put on the G suits to see how much they helped. In my case they increased my tolerance about one G; this, of course, differs among pilots according to their physical make-up.

After improving the cockpit and making the pilot more comfortable, we turned our attention to his problems if he had to leave the airplane in flight. No longer was it possible simply to climb over the side and jump out; the force of air in a jet going 600 miles an hour would blast him back against the tail and bash him to bits. What was needed was a device to propel him from the plane with sufficient force to clear the tail surfaces; this led us to the ejection seat as we know it today.

Parallel with the pilot escape problem, we worked on a program to improve his parachute. The old seat-type chute could no longer be used with ejection seats, because it failed at high speeds. After many tests we found that a backtype chute would stand up better and afford the same protection; development of the new chute is still continuing to make it more acceptable, but in the meantime it fills the need.

Jet speed also presented new problems of navigation. The pilot flying 600 miles an hour needed instruments to give him his position, altitude, and heading at all times. If he had to land in darkness or bad weather, he also needed instruments that could guide him safely to the ground. This was especially important for jet fighters, with their limited fuel capacity and high fuel consumption. To overcome these problems, we worked on several programs at the same time.

Ground-Controlled Approach, or GCA, which uses a ground observer and radar to talk the pilot down to the runway, was first tried out at Wright Field; I helped set up and standardize its procedures. ILS, the Instrument Landing System, was also coming into its own, with the pilot guiding himself to the field through a visual presentation in the cockpit. We ran many tests on the ILS system during its development years.

Another new requirement was an improved radio compass. With the early F-80 and F-84 jets, where accurate navigation was essential to a successful mission, we insisted on a radio compass as standard equipment. I remember taking off many times with a low ceiling, below minimum, provided that skies were clear above the overcast, and returning and landing with the aid of a radio compass. We lost some flying time because of bad weather, but improved navigation aids kept it to a minimum.

As jet speeds increased the pilot found it difficult to control the airplane with his arms and legs. Increased air pressures on the control surfaces at high speeds were too great for human muscles. Beginning with the F-80, hydraulic boost systems were installed in all our jets to aid the manual controls. We ran many tests on different types of power-boosted controls, such as the completely irreversible control system on the F-86E. As aircraft speeds continue to increase, the problem of controlling the airplane is becoming paramount.

With the first flight of the F-86 Sabre Jet in 1948, America's first sweptwing airplane came into being. The application of this German theory to an American plane was a giant step forward in aircraft design in the United States, as it was elsewhere throughout the world. It gave us a tactical airplane with performance appreciably greater than that of earlier straight-wing jets. By sweeping the wings back at an angle from the fuselage, drag was reduced, permitting the plane to fly faster.

To me the 86 was a dream airplane. You would notice that it took off and landed with nose-high attitude, because the shape of the wings reduced their lift and required a greater angle of attack to compensate for it. The first three airplanes had an Allison J-35 engine, also used in the F-84; with the same power plant, the performance increase of the newer plane was not too great. But later planes had the new General Electric J-47 engine with more power, and their performance increased accordingly.

Using this engine, the F-86 soundly whipped the swept-wing MIG-15 Russian jet in Korea and set new records for speed. Today nearly all our new jet fighters and bombers have sweptback wings. The only exception is the F-104 Starfighter, a straight-wing airplane which is an entirely new theory exploited by Kelly Johnson of Lockheed.

With the design and production of new jet airplanes, we also tested new and more powerful engines. In those days the jet engine was just beginning to grow. The first Allison J-33 in the early F-80 delivered about 3,000 pounds of thrust, compared to 15,000 pounds in present production engines. We ran various tests in constant efforts to get more power. We injected water alcohol into the burner cans to increase thrust on take-off. When Allison perfected the J-35 engine for the F-84 we gained more thrust through improved design.

The axial-flow engine gets more thrust from ram air coming through the intake ducts. With this thrust increase, we could reduce fuel consumption and increase range accordingly. Or we could put on more power and fly faster. The jet engine also brought with it a new fuel, basically a purified kerosene. Because it was expensive to make, we constantly flew tests to find cheaper blends that would provide the same operating efficiency. From these tests we finally standardized on JP-4, a mixture of kerosene and gasoline that is used most commonly today.

In the early days we were trying to make the jet acceptable

to fly under any operating conditions. To be practical and useful, it had to work equally well in any part of the world and in all kinds of weather. To test it under cold-weather conditions, we set up a cold-weather test detachment at Ladd Field, near Fairbanks, Alaska, shortly after the war, and spent the winter months flying tests in a cold climate.

I spent the winter of 1947-1948 at Ladd Field as assistant chief of the detachment, testing a P-51, two F-80's, an F-84, a B-50, and two T-6's with magnesium wings. We ran into problems with both the jets and their fuel. For example, we found that JP fuel dripping on the rubber tires during the day caused them to soften and lose their shape. Then at night they would freeze and harden. The next morning when the pilot started down the runway he would have a tire with a flat spot in it, a dangerous condition when taking off or landing. As a result of our experience the tire manufacturers have improved the rubber to withstand a fuel reaction.

Another serious problem was fuel sludging. The fuel would freeze in subzero temperatures and form tiny ice crystals that

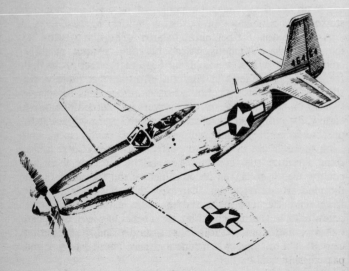

P-51 Mustang

clogged the filters and caused engine flameouts resulting from fuel starvation. Working with Lockheed, who manufactured the F-80, we solved the problem by installing an automatic pump to deliver alcohol to the filter and melt the ice particles whenever they formed. We lost several pilots before we licked the problem, but that was part of the job in the early days of jet testing.

In December, 1948, I was sent to the North American Aviation plant at Los Angeles to pick up one of the new F-86 jets and ferry it back to Dayton. Up to this time I had not flown the new sweptwing plane, which was less than a year old. However, it had passed its first test and was approved for cross-country operations.

Before leaving Wright Field I received a thorough briefing on the airplane from experienced pilots. I got a cockpit check from George Welch, North American's chief test pilot, upon reaching Los Angeles. Th airplane looked fine. I started the engine, waved good-by to George, and took off for Ohio. With the range available in those days, I could expect to fly about 500 miles before refueling. However, my orders were vague on this point, and the number and location of refueling stops were optional.

As I tucked up the wheels and started my climb to altitude, the California mountains passed beneath me and ahead I could see the brown waste of the Mojave Desert. At 40,000 feet I leveled off and applied full throttle. Effortlessly the shiny little airplane accelerated up to its maximum speed. Flying at Mach .9, I rolled it over and turned the nose earthward, pulling on through in a split S and continuing to pick up speed as my dive momentum increased.

Now the airplane began to buffet as it entered the transsonic zone and the steady whine of the air flow over the cockpit rose in pitch. At Mach .96, near the speed of sound, the plane shook its wings sharply, like a dog shaking water from its back. The right rudder buffeted briefly as compressibility seized the tail surfaces. Then I saw my air speed indicator and altimeter needle spin rapidly and the buffeting ceased. The cockpit was suddenly quiet and I knew I had passed the sound barrier.

Except for the hiss of air over the canopy, all noise was

behind me. I felt both awed and proud. The silent airplane was flashing toward the ground at 1,000 feet a second. Now it was time to pull out of the dive. At 20,000 feet I went to work on the controls, careful not to overstress the airplane, and slowly my headlong plunge slackened as the nose lifted toward the eastern horizon. In level flight again, I turned toward the landing field at Muroc Air Base, now visible in the distance. It wasn't 500 miles from Los Angeles, but there was nothing in my orders that said I couldn't stop there. Besides, I wanted to celebrate my first supersonic flight.

During my four years at Wright Field, I met and worked with many of aviation's leading civilian pilots. Like George Welch and Dan Darnell at North American, most of them tested airplanes for aircraft manufacturers to make a living; some flew in air races on the side—men like Tony LeVier and Fish Salmon of Lockheed; Jack Woolams and Skip Ziegler of Bell; and Tex Johnston of Bell, now chief of flight test at Boeing. They were leaders in their profession and I looked up to them for guidance and inspiration.

On the other hand, many civilians looked down upon the military test pilot. A newcomer since World War II, he was inexperienced in comparison to men who had been flying and testing new airplanes for fifteen and twenty years. For the most part, we did not question their position. They got all the rough jobs—the first flights, the structural demonstrations, the spin tests and high-speed dives. It is true that they were paid well, considering the risks they took, but the fact remained that they did the work. As a result we took their leadership for granted.

This relationship began to change when Chuck Yeager broke the sound barrier in October, 1947. The future of military flight testing was riding with him that morning in the little X-1. Colonel Boyd, who supervised the project, was aware that many people felt we were too inexperienced for the assignment, one which no civilian pilot had yet accomplished. Had Yeager failed it would have confirmed the warnings of our worst critics, and for this reason we moved very cautiously. But Chuck's successful flight did much more than silence criticism. It opened the way for the military test pilot to accept more responsibility and participate as an equal in the future development of aviation.

The X-1 to me was a goal that appeared to be far beyond my reach. There were several pilots ahead of me on the list to fly it, all with more seniority and testing experience. I asked questions and discussed the test program with them. But for me the rocket airplane as such remained an unattainable ambition.

In January, 1949, Dick Johnson became chief of the fighter test section at Wright Field and I was named his assistant. A few months later the Air Materiel Command activated Muroc as a new Air Force flight test center and Colonel Boyd went to California as its first commanding officer. For those of us who were staying behind, his departure was a personal misfortune. An inspiration to all who knew him, through his example and leadership he personified for us all that was good and important in the Air Force.

He demanded the utmost in proficiency, and any time he felt that we were not far above average in our aggressive attitude and our ability to fly, he was sure to mention it. Mistakes were not tolerated; any pilot who erred could expect to receive a good chewing out, and if the error was repeated, Colonel Boyd would take steps to have him transferred. But when we did a good job he was always complimentary, and if we had trouble and came out of it unscathed and in a commendable manner, he made a point of telling us.

He was a pilot's pilot. He flew constantly himself, in any kind of airplane, any time and anywhere; he was always flying jets with us and knew what we were talking about when we ran into trouble. He would never send any of us up on a flight or in bad weather unless he could or would have done it himself. When we ran afoul of regulations, we could always depend upon him to go to bat for us if we were worthy of it. His loyalty to us was far-reaching and of course our loyalty to him was returned in like manner. I didn't know of anyone who wasn't highly loyal to him and ready to do anything for him. We could always depend upon Colonel Boyd to stand behind us, and we grew to respect and love him dearly.

6

X-1

Early in January, 1949, Colonel Albert Boyd, chief of the flight test division at Wright Field, Ohio, called me to his office for an interview. At this time I was devoting full time to test work on jet fighter aircraft, so I assumed that he wished to discuss some of the programs we had laid out for improving these planes and getting new models into service.

His secretary announced me, I walked in and saluted, and he asked me to sit down. Then he hitched his chair up squarely facing me and came directly to the point.

It concerned a rocket ship, not jets—the famous Bell X-1. This was the aircraft that Captain Charles Yeager had flown faster than sound in October, 1947, in man's first supersonic flight. Since that time, Chuck and several other pilots, military and civilian, had broken the sound barrier in this airplane. In September, 1948, Air Force Secretary Symington stated publicly that it had flown several hundred miles faster than sound. Of course I knew about its performance and was well aware that maximum speed for the original model had probably been reached. My only regret was that I had not yet had the opportunity to fly it.

There were no more records to be set—speed records, that is. But altitude records were another matter. And that was why I was here in Colonel Boyd's office. The Air Force wanted to run altitude tests on the X-1, he told me, and he asked if I cared to undertake this hazardous mission. If possible we hoped to break the existing world's altitude record, which was held by an Army balloon at 72,000 feet.

More important, we would get valuable information on aircraft performance at high altitudes—information not now available because jet and propeller-driven planes could not go high enough. A whole new world waited to be explored by a powered aircraft—the air world above 50,000 feet. If a rocket ship could reach it—and he believed it could—the secrets of the unknown stratosphere now lay open to powered flight. For the first time we could discover how a manned vehicle would behave at high speeds in the upper air. It was even possible that some day we could fly still higher beyond the earth's atmosphere.

To me the opportunity was a challenge to explore, and I accepted without a moment's hesitation. I was almost speechless with excitement and anticipation. Colonel Boyd attempted to slow me down. He tried to impress upon me the importance of this program, as well as the hazards. He did not want any happy-go-lucky test pilot going out and doing a haphazard job that might embarrass the Air Force. Did I understand the need for approaching it carefully and scientifically? More to the point, was I prepared to conduct the altitude program in a careful and scientific manner?

Finding it extremely hard to control my enthusiasm, I assured him that I was. Apparently my attitude was satisfactory, because I was told to go ahead and plan on flying the tests. This meant a temporary assignment to Muroc Air Force Base, the X-1 test site in the California desert near Los Angeles. The oversize landing field on Rogers Dry Lake at Muroc, more than 15 miles of natural runway, was the safest place to make the deadstick landings required in the X-1. I might be gone several months, so I should plan on taking my family. Vicky was only two and Cindy, the baby, just a few months old, but my wife thought the desert would be a healthy place for children, so she too was eager to make the move.

My first step was a visit to the Aero-Medical branch at Wright Field, where I learned to wear the new high-altitude pressure suit Chuck Yeager had pioneered in the X-1. This was still in the developmental stage and had not yet been tried out in a real emergency, as we had never experienced an explosive decompression in an aircraft at dangerous heights. However, I would be flying above 63,000 feet, where my blood would boil if the cockpit pressure failed, and the pressure suit was one of those things you had to take along.

I underwent tests in the pressure chamber at Wright Field, where high-altitude conditions can be simulated on the ground. I visited the manufacturer at Worcester, Massachusetts, to have a new suit designed and built to my own size. Back at Wright Field again, I practiced wearing it and getting used to it in the cockpit of an airplane, while medical officers observed my reactions under operating conditions.

The suit was very uncomfortable, even though it was made to my own measurements. The tight-fitting garment constricted my movements and the tight laces impeded the circulation of blood in my arms and legs. Worse still, it was almost airtight, and when wearing it I sweated profusely, even in cold weather. Although I was in good physical condition, I usually finished a test run several pounds below my take-off weight.

Although the suit was bad, the pressure helmet we wore at that time was even worse. It had to fit tightly to maintain an air seal, and as a result it became quite painful after any length of time. The longest I could stand it was about an hour before the pressures created by the helmet and the suit would overcome me and I was ready to give up.

But despite the discomforts I knew the X-1 would be worth it. I was so eager to fly it I would have worn a suit four times as bad. When I had learned to live and work in high-altitude clothing and passed a thorough medical examination to make certain that I was physically qualified, I was given final approval to proceed with the altitude tests. Early in March, after nearly two months of intensive preparations, I packed up my family and drove west.

When I reported in to Muroc, a little test section detachment from Wright Field was already operating at the desert air base. Bell and a few other manufacturers had some people out there, but altogether they were a mere handful compared to the thousands today who have turned the desert into a modern city. I reported to Major Bob Cardenas, the bomber pilot commanding the flight test detachment, who flew the B-29 used to carry the X-1 aloft on its test flights. Also on hand to greet us were Chuck Yeager, Jack Ridley, the X-1 flight test engineer, and other Wright Field acquaintances.

As my next assignment I studied the X-1 until I became thoroughly familiar with its operation. Although I had seen the little rocket ship many times, I had never had occasion to study it. I went through a ground school conducted by Yeager and Ridley, aided by Dick Frost, the Bell Aircraft Corporation engineer in charge of the X-1 project. After I was thoroughly briefed on the rocket engine, the first of its kind in this country, I made several ground runs to test my knowledge of the system and to observe the engine in actual operation.

The X-1, first airplane in the world to exceed the speed of sound in level flight, was also America's first rocket-powered aircraft. It was laid down in 1944, five years before I flew it, as a wartime research project of the Army Air Forces. The contract called for a minimum speed of 800 miles an hour for two to five minutes at 35,000 feet or above. Although it was a research airplane, the configuration and controls were conventional. But its engine was a unique power plant which began a whole new age of flight.

Designed by a then unknown company, Reaction Motors, for an unknown Navy plane that had not yet flown, the X-1 engine was a pioneering development in every sense of the word. The design of the engine, four rocket tubes mounted in a cluster, had never been used before in an airplane. The fuel, a mixture of water alcohol and liquid oxygen, had never been employed in powered flight. Forced into the rocket chambers under very high pressure by nitrogen gas, their combustion produced a forward thrust of 6,000 pounds. In the little X-1, which weighed only 6,200 pounds empty, this was enough to drive it 120,000 feet high at a maximum speed of nearly 1,400 miles an hour.

In later models of the airplane there was a steam-driven turbine pump to force the propellants into the rocket engine. But like everything else about this power plant, the pump had never been built before, and we did not wait for it. The nitrogen pressure system which was used in the first airplane cut down by nearly one-half the amount of fuel it could carry, reducing its flight time correspondingly, but it permitted the project to move ahead.

In the decade since the first powered flight of the X-1 in December, 1946, rocket engines have carried man to speeds and heights not possible with any other power plant. Rockets have made the whole new field of guided missiles and earth satellites a reality. Beyond this we already are planning the rocket engines that will power manned space vehicles and interplanetary flights. Truly, the little makeshift power plant that first sent the X-1 shooting skyward brought a new era in human knowledge and achievement.

On March 21, 1949, I made my first flight in the X-1. Like several that followed, it was strictly a familiarization flight, and except for the thrill of flying a rocket airplane, was fairly routine. I practiced firing the rocket chambers, alternately and in sequence, feeling the blast of power behind me as the engine came to life. But I had been instructed to hold the speed down at first and I did not go supersonic. Mostly I was feeling the airplane out and getting acquainted with the way it flew.

Four days later, on my second flight, I went supersonic in the X-1. It was on this flight that I experienced a rocket fire and automatic shutdown resulting from a leaking fuel valve. Because of damage caused by this accident, the test program was delayed for engine repairs and I did not fly the X-1 again until April 19.

We had agreed with the Bell people that, starting with my third flight, I would attempt to go for maximum altitude. But again we experienced engine trouble, as I could get only two rocket chambers firing, and as a result I had to turn back at 60,000 feet. We had a lot of difficulty in those days starting the rocket chamber igniters that lighted the propellants.

On this flight I was bothered by a head cold which caused a pressure on my eardrums. After rocket burnout, while I was gliding down to land, the pressure in my ears became very painful, and the only way I could relieve it was to hold my nose and blow.

However, I was wearing an old-type pressure helmet with fixed visor, which could not be opened. Helmets developed later have a hinged facepiece the pilot can lift up. Nor could I remove my helmet with its supply of life-saving oxygen, for the cockpit was filled with deadly nitrogen gas used to pressurize the cockpit. So there I was and that was the way I had to stay. It was only a matter of seconds before my eardrum let go, and suffering considerable pain I came on down and landed.

Medical examination revealed that damage was minor, as the rupture was small, and a week or two later, after the hole had healed over and become strong enough to withstand pressure, I resumed my test work in the X-1.

As a result of this accident, I began carrying an extra helmet with me—the regular crash helmet I normally used in flying. Any time I had ear trouble I would rip off the pressure helmet, hold my nose, and blow hard, thus relieving the pressure in my ears. Taking care not to inhale the nitrogen gas in the cockpit, I then hurriedly donned the crash helmet, which I could plug into the X-1 oxygen system.

I was making my letdown on a subsequent flight when again my ears started to hurt. Without really thinking about what I was doing, I ripped off the pressure helmet, blew my nose, and put on my crash hat. To do this I had to let go of the wheel and use two hands, and in the meantime the X-1 rolled over on its back.

I was holding my breath, in a hurry to plug in my oxygen tube and also get the airplane right side up again. After two or three breaths I felt that I was suffocating. I was aware of a prickling sensation in my arms and legs and I felt strange all over. My hands lost control and began to jerk about the cockpit and I could not hold my head up.

Thinking there must be something wrong with the oxygen system, I reached down and released the emergency oxygen supply fitted to my parachute. Eternities passed before my fumbling fingers found the precious bail-out bottle. As my mask flooded with life-saving oxygen, I looked around the cockpit, and then I saw that I had plugged my breathing tube into the nitrogen outlet.

With trembling hands I pulled the tube out and plugged it in correctly. Then I came in and landed without further trouble. But I was very shaken by the knowledge of my foolhardy mistake, and for a long time I did not mention it to anyone because I was ashamed to admit my error.

The X-1 had gone back in the shop for repairs after my third flight and two weeks elapsed before I flew it again. This was another attempt to reach maximum altitude. After dropping from the B-29 I started three rocket chambers and began climbing, when suddenly I felt and heard a sharp explosion in the rear of the airplane, and at the same time all three rocket chambers shut down.

I tried to move the rudder but it was locked in position. I was unable to see the rear of the plane, to determine the reason, and there was no help from my chase pilot, who by this time was out of sight far below. But I did not have a fire warning light in the cockpit, so I reported over the radio as calmly as I could that I had experienced another engine explosion and shutdown and was returning to base.

I glided back to the dry lake bed, jettisoning my remaining fuel as I came down from altitude, and flying with the rudder locked. At 30,000 feet my F-80 chase plane caught up with me. Dick Frost, flying chase that day, moved in close behind to take a look at the engine compartment, and in a moment he came on the air to report that my No. 1 rocket chamber had blown up. The rudder had been damaged by the explosion and would not move.

I landed without difficulty, using my brakes to maintain directional control, and came to a normal halt. But upon inspection of the airplane, it was found that damage was considerable. Exhaust from the No. 2 and No. 3 rocket chambers had ignited gases from the No. 1 chamber and as the fire moved back inside, the propellants had blown up. Again the rocket igniter that failed to light was responsible for the malfunction, but this time damage was so extensive that the airplane had to be returned to Wright Field for major repairs.

In July the airplane was brought back to Muroc and I made my fifth flight in the X-1. It was not too successful. Again we encountered trouble with the rocket igniters, and again the little airplane went back to the shop for repair and modifications. With the engine functioning properly once more, early in August I took the X-1 up for the sixth time.

At the preflight briefing the preceding afternoon, we agreed on a dawn take-off for another assault on the world's altitude record. In the interval between darkness and daylight, winds are calm over the quiet desert, creating the best conditions for rocket launching; and at that time of day, when normal flying activity is at a minimum, our little rocket ship shooting skyward like a bullet would present the least hazard to other aircraft that might be aloft over Southern California.

I went to bed early after dinner, hoping to get a sound night's rest. The children were asleep and Avis also retired early. Sensing my strain, and wishing to help me prepare for the coming ordeal, she refrained from talking after we turned the lights off, and soon she fell asleep.

Not so with me. I lay awake in the quiet house a long time, my thoughts on the coming flight, and my mind rehearsing over and over the plans for its execution. Mentally I went over again each step in the flight plan, beginning with the take-off in the B-29. I was vividly aware of the many hazards and unknowns that lay before me. Lighting a fresh cigarette from the burning stub of another, I smoked and tossed as the hours passed until long after midnight.

I had not been asleep very long when the alarm clock shrilled in the darkness, waking me suddenly from restless dreams. Avis too awoke and called over to me. Shaking my head to clear away fatigue, I rose slowly to my feet and made myself ready for the coming day.

When I had finished dressing, Avis had breakfast waiting for me—a light meal of grapefruit, oatmeal, and milk. I am not much of a breakfast man under any circumstances, and hunger leaves me entirely in time of stress. Through the shaded window to the east I could see the first slivers of morning breaking across the blackness of the desert sky. Breakfast over, I tiptoed into the nursery for a look at the sleeping children. Avis followed me on to the porch and as she kissed me good-by and told me to be careful, I was aware of a special urgency and concern in her voice. I winked at her and said, "No sweat."

When I reached the flight line the B-29 sat waiting in the semidarkness, its strange cargo already fastened in its belly on the ground. Air Force officers would pilot both planes, but otherwise the X-1 was still a Bell company project, and civilian engineers and mechanics prepared them for flight. The ground crew were still loading propellants into the X-1, exotic and dangerous fuels made of water alcohol and liquid oxygen. Other personnel were checking the intricate instruments the X-1 carried and making a final inspection of its power plant and controls.

Standing near the airplane with Jack Ridley, the flight engineer, and Dick Frost, the project engineer, I once more went over last-minute instructions for the flight. Chuck Yeager would fly chase plane for me today, and with him I reviewed again emergency procedures in event of trouble. Bob Cardenas, the B-29 pilot, joined us shortly, and we discussed with him the familiar plan for climb and drop.

Mornings at Edwards are hot in August, and I was perspiring as Dave Mahoney, the Aero-Medical officer responsible for much of our new high-altitude equipment, helped me get into my pressure suit. I wore heavy winter underwear beneath it to keep it from chafing and pinching, and the combination of both garments made me uncomfortably warm. Then I put on the pressure helmet, which Dave helped me check out by blowing oxygen into the helmet through the suit. The helmet was uncomfortable too, and I took it off as soon as possible and carried it in my hand as I got on board the B-29.

At 7,000 feet Major Cardenas indicated that it was time for me to enter the cockpit of the X-1. I put my helmet on once more, pulled on a pair of silk-lined leather gloves, and Jack Ridley helped me into a wool-and-nylon flying coat over my pressure suit. Fully dressed now, I entered the bomb bay and stepped aboard the one-man elevator that lowered me to the opening in the side of the rocket plane.

The slipstream was buffeting me and the bomber's four 3,500-horsepower engines were howling in my ears. If the elevator broke there was nothing between me and the ground— not even a parachute. Feeling trapped and nervous, I struggled through the small door into the X-1 cockpit and slipped sideways into my seat. I was completely exhausted by the ordeal, and despite my heavy clothing I was cold already. The parachute was in the seat and I strapped it on as I sat down. As I fastened my seat and shoulder harness I felt tired from lack of oxygen and the long period of waiting for the flight to begin.

Squirming in the cramped cockpit to settle myself in the most comfortable position, I plugged in my oxygen mask and bail-out bottle and connected my headset and microphone to the X-1's radio cord. Major Cardenas and I exchanged a few words to test my radio communications. As they appeared satisfactory, I told Jack Ridley I was ready to seal the cockpit. I helped him pull the metal door into place, locking it from the inside and checking to make certain it was secured properly. Then I signaled with my hand and he climbed back into the B-29.

As he pulled the little aluminum elevator up into the mother ship I was left completely isolated in my cubicle, alone and shut away from any other humans. I felt a pang of loneliness, although I could see Ridley and his companions peering down at me through the X-1 windshield, and once or twice I motioned to them in the bomb bay of the B-29.

But this feeling passed as quickly as it had come, and now I busied myself with the long list of controls and instruments to be checked before my flight. Although it would be nearly forty-five minutes before we reached drop altitude at 30,000 feet, there was plenty of work to be done. Back of me in the X-1 the white vapor trails trailing off behind the airplane marked the liquid oxygen constantly boiling away as the B-29 continued its climb.

As we neared drop altitude the top-off crew in the bomber began refilling the liquid oxygen tanks. The highly volatile liquid burned at the rate of 125 gallons a minute under maximum power, and every gallon would be precious in the coming flight. At five minutes to drop, Major Cardenas called Chuck Yeager over the radio to take up his chase plane position. Looking back over my right shoulder, I could see his F-80 jet off to the right as he made ready to observe my drop and engine start.

Now I checked my fuel jettison system, releasing a short burst of water alcohol and liquid oxygen to make certain the valves were operating. If my rocket engine failed to start, I would be unable to land the X-1 with three tons of explosive propellants on board. Then I checked my controls, moving the ailerons and tail surfaces manually, and Yeager advised me from his F-80 that they appeared to be working properly.

At one minute to drop the tension increased. I calibrated and zeroed my instruments, turned on the instrument switches and photo panel switches, and also checked my cockpit camera and turned it on. A last look around the cockpit, a last check of my pressure and oxygen outlets, and I reached forward with my right hand and switched on the launch-ready light.

As I did so a green light glowed in the cockpit of the B-29, and Major Cardenas pushed the big bomber over into a shallow dive. On his airspeed indicator the needle crept slowly up to 250 miles an hour as his speed increased. Then it was only ten seconds to drop, and over the intercom he began his count-down in a loud and clear voice:

"Ten—nine—eight—seven—six—five—four—three—two—one—DROP!"

I was tense as I dropped from the shadowed belly of the B-29 into the dazzling brightness of a new day. The motion was abrupt, as if a giant hand had thrown me away from the mother ship, and the X-1 fell like a stone earthward.

Still falling, my fingers moved instinctively over and closed on the toggle switches to fire the rocket chambers in the silent plane. Quickly I depressed the switches in rapid succession. As if a monster sledge hammer had struck the cockpit behind me, I was forced back in my seat as three chambers ignited in a blast of deafening power. I gasped for breath in my deflated lungs while my hands slowly pulled the control wheel back toward my chest and the nose of the X-1 pointed skyward.

Now the B-29 was behind and far below me as the fiery furnace of burning propellants hurled me upward. Catching my breath at last, I spoke with effort over the radio. "Three chambers firing," I said deliberately, maintaining a calm and even voice so I could be understood by the listeners on the ground. Still climbing with me but rapidly falling behind, Chuck Yeager in the F-80 chase plane came on the air to confirm my engine start. "Everything looks fine from here," he assured me.

I was alone now, but hardly conscious of my surroundings, as I held the nose of the soaring rocket ship in a steep climb upward. The control wheel moved impulsively in my hands and my grip instinctively tightened to steady it as the rushing air blasted against the hurtling plane. My eyes were concentrated on the air speed indicator and my arms strained achingly against the control surfaces as I strove to hold the climb angle that would keep my upward rush at the predetermined speed.

A mere flick of my eye muscles, no more than the fraction of a second, showed me altitude was already 45,000 feet.

Now ever so slowly, ever so carefully, I pushed forward on the wheel to nose over into level flight. A glance at the Machmeter and then back to the altimeter. Speed now was Mach .9—nine-tenths of the speed of sound. The upward rush of the airplane continued and accelerated as it passed 50,000 feet.

Now I beeped the stabilizer to nose-down position as I prepared to go supersonic. Between Mach .9 and Mach 1, I again felt the airplane buffet moderately to severely as the shock waves increased. Then the buffet suddenly slackened and my eyes again swept the three crucial dials that guided me on my solitary and headlong journey. I saw the jump and rise in the Machmeter and the air-speed and altimeter gauges, and the hurtling airplane, grown suddenly silent as noise itself was outdistanced, lunged irresistibly beyond the speed of sound.

Now I reached down and turned off my Machmeter. Still a crude makeshift instrument, it was not designed to operate at extreme altitudes. The altimeter stood at 55,000 feet. I was aware of the absence of sound in the cockpit, broken only by the static of the radio in the headset, as I pointed the nose of the X-1 skyward again and switched on the fourth rocket chamber for the final portion of my climb.

Sound could not tell me it did not start, for all sound was behind me. Only from the blank eye on the chamber pressure gauge, a dot of emptiness in the shadowy cockpit, did I know the fourth chamber was not firing. But there was no time to speculate on the reason for the malfunction. X-1 rocket time was critical, measured in seconds, and my job now was to fly on three chambers to maximum altitude before the fuel was gone.

The altimeter lag, at least 5,000 feet at my present rate of climb, was automatically discounted and taken into consideration. Once more my attention was fixed on the air-speed indicator, the one remaining instrument I had left to fly the plane. The thrust of the rocket engine was now almost as great as the weight of the airplane as I rushed upward in a nearly vertical climb. I cranked in a little aileron and attempted to pull back on the wheel, endeavouring to maintain positive G or the normal pull of gravity on the plane. The controls were sluggish, especially the elevators and stabilizer, and the control column moved loosely in its track without effect on the path of flight.

I felt the sudden decrease in forward thrust as the operating rocket chambers, their fuel supply exhausted, abruptly burned themselves out and shut down. There was a sharp deceleration and I was pushed up in my shoulder harness tight against the straps. Speed was Mach 1.3 and altitude over 65,000 feet. Hurled skyward by the vast momentum of its climb, though without any internal power to support it, the X-1 still flashed upward in supersonic flight.

At rocket burn-out I glanced outside the cockpit for the first time. My feeling was one of eerie loneliness in the silent little plane. Glancing up at the sky toward which it still carried me with unbelievable force, I saw a dome of deep, dark purple, unlike any color I had ever known on the ground. Far, far below me, a mote in space, was the earth I lived on, flat and featureless, except at the horizon, where I could see the curve of the great globe itself.

Still climbing as I was, the airplane suddenly began to buffet, and I knew it was nearing a stall. The rate of climb was less now, but the altimeter needle still crept higher, and I estimated my altitude over 70,000 feet. I attempted to keep the nose pointed upward, but the airplane reacted like a ballistic missile as its remaining momentum began to spend itself, and slowly the nose started its movement downward toward level flight.

At the top of the long arc that would lead me earthward the X-1 paused momentarily, shuddered like a spent bird, then settled downward. I was still flying forward, though my headlong momentum had slackened, but the unwinding altimeter told me I was falling toward the ground.

The silent airplane was still in a nose-high position as it fell. Then the nose dropped slowly down to level flight. There was no time now to speculate on whether I had established a new altitude record, as my instruments later indicated. There were other tests to make, abrupt pull-ups to reach accelerated stall condition at supersonic speed, and flying the airplane once more I pushed the X-1 over in a steep dive.

Again the air-speed indicator moved upward, until at 63,000 feet and Mach 1.1, I pulled sharply back on the control wheel and cranked in full nose-up stabilizer. Now let's see what happens. The nose moved slowly up to the horizon and suddenly the X-1 stalled, bucking and snap-rolling and pitching violently before I could get the stabilizer into nose-down position again. Then abruptly as they had begun the wild gyrations ceased, and in control of the airplane again, I dumped the nose once more in another steep dive.

Now it was all routine. Pick up speed in a dive, then pull up till the airplane begins to stall out, then over and down again in another dive. I did several pull-ups, at the highest dive speed possible without losing too much altitude, down to around 30,000 feet. This kind of flying was fun! Then over the radio Chuck Yeager gave me my heading, and once more my chase plane had me in sight.

We let down together toward the dry lake bed, his F-80 behind and slightly below me, talking me toward the ground. I had a dead engine and the X-1 was not a tactical airplane, but at 5,000 feet I did a regular tactical approach. At 300 miles per hour indicated, I peeled off and dumped the landing gear in the little airplane. Then base leg, dump the flaps, final approach, and I was home.

We never claimed the world's altitude record officially, because the instruments we had for measuring altitude in those days were not very accurate. However, we still were confident that we had surpassed the previous record of 72,000 feet by at least 1,000 feet. And I felt very good about having flown to a height no man had reached before.

When flying the X-1, I was always quite busy trying to maintain the proper climb schedule to gain desired altitude with minimum fuel consumption. Part of the job, in fact, was to establish what this climb speed should be.

In the transsonic zone between Mach .9 and Mach 1, the airplane was subjected to high buffet, and the best method to get out of this region had to be determined by actual testing. If a constant climb speed was maintained to altitude before going supersonic, the airplane was subjected to considerable buffeting, which was inefficient; on the other hand, a supersonic climb, while a lot smoother, also burned up fuel much faster.

Finally after many test flights and studying the data results, we hit on a compromise climb condition. The first part was subsonic flight to 45,000 feet, traveling at Mach .8 increasing to .9. We buffeted in the region between .9 and Mach 1; leveled out around 45,000 feet and became supersonic; then pulled the nose up sharply and climbed supersonically until reaching altitude, which in the tests I was running meant the highest I could go.

This was the ideal climb schedule. However, the X-1 had conventional control surfaces, including an adjustable stabilizer that was not designed for very high speeds, and as a result I was always quite busy flying the airplane and usually had little time left to worry about a proper climb.

The X-1 was a small airplane, weighing only 6,200 pounds empty, and as the fuel burned off, the amount of engine thrust would approach the total weight of the airplane. As a result, I would usually end up climbing almost vertically while my speed continued to increase. Climbing like this at a steep angle, it was impossible to see the ground from the cockpit, and this lack of visual reference further increased the problem of holding a steady climb path.

This steep climb angle also presented another problem. It was not hazardous, as there was no danger involved to me or the airplane, but if trouble did occur, it could result in a rocket shutdown. This problem arose from the fuel feed system to the rocket engine from the propellant tanks.

The fuel lines to the engine came out of the bottom of the tanks. Near the end of the climb to altitude, with the X-1 in a steep angle upward, these tanks would be nearly empty, and the remaining fuel was back in the rear of the tanks. To compensate for this condition and make sure the fuel would continue flowing from tanks to engine, it was necessary to maintain a positive G on the airplane through centrifugal force by pulling back on the wheel in a sort of spiralling climb. Unless this was done, the fuel would slosh around in the tanks, and even a slight negative G, or antigravity force, would cause the propellant to rise from the bottom of the tanks. As it did so it would uncover the fuel ports and the engine would immediately shut down.

In doing the altitude flights we were attempting to reach the highest altitude possible, and even after rocket shutdown I would permit the X-1 to continue climbing in a gliding manner under its own momentum. However, immediately upon shutdown the airplane began to decelerate. The small amount of engine noise and vibration in the cockpit disappeared and I had an odd feeling of being all alone by myself up above the earth, with no one else around. The chase pilots were far below me, and I had this strange feeling of being far beyond the reach of any other human being.

It was impossible for us in those days to determine the exact altitude we reached. The X-1 was equipped with a crude altimeter that gave altitude markings in tens of thousands of feet up to 80,000 feet, but it was very inadequate. The airplane also carried a standard altimeter that gave closer measurements but it would not read above 50,000 feet. The Machmeter also had to be turned off around 50,000 feet, as it was not designed to function at higher altitudes. As a result, speed as well as height were pretty much guesswork in those days when you went any distance up in the sky.

I have been asked by many people if I weren't frightened on these flights and subjected to unusual mental stress. I must truthfully reply that I was not. There is a constant feeling of apprehension on all test flights, because the pilot is fully aware of the hazards involved, both known and unknown. Moreover, he is naturally concerned with his responsibilities for the safekeeping of an expensive vehicle which is extremely important to the Air Force and the manufacturer. These things naturally worried me. But I did not feel fear as such.

I had been thoroughly briefed on the X-1 and what I could expect from it. Wind tunnel studies and the experience of other pilots helped me to predict much of its behavior and gave me confidence resulting from known facts. Of course we were not too sure what would happen if it stalled out at high altitude after reaching its maximum height. We believed it possible the airplane would start tumbling out of control and re-enter the denser atmosphere at lower altitudes at a high rate of speed.

If this happened before the pilot could regain control, and the airplane entered the dense air in a flat position that would subject it to high stresses, we considered it entirely possible that both the airplane and the pilot might be destroyed. Of course, we found out several years later through actual experience in another model that even when the X-1 went out of control, they both survived.

What fear I felt I like to explain as the fear of competition. In the X-1, I was competing against the elements for my life and thus the stakes were the highest. But otherwise it was like any competition for me; it was the same feeling I had had on a football field before the kickoff or waiting for the bell to ring on the first round of a boxing match. It was a competitive fear, and I always went through the most apprehensive moments in the X-1 just before the game started—that is, before I dropped from the belly of the B-29. My stomach knotted up, especially during countdown, and I sometimes held my breath waiting for the drop. But once I dropped and was on my own again, I felt relaxed and at ease and reacted normally throughout the rest of the flight.

Flying the X-1 was serious business, but along with the worries and troubles we also had our share of laughs. Jack Ridley was up one morning on a check flight, with Chuck Yeager and I chasing him in F-80 jets. He had dropped from the B-29 and flown for a minute or two when he called out in his high, nasal, Oklahoma twang that he had a fire in the cockpit. Of course we knew it could only be an electrical fire, as there was nothing else there to burn.

Chuck and I wanted to save the X-1 at all costs, as it meant a great deal to both of us, so we immediately came on the air to assure him that he was not in any danger.

"Relax, Jack, it's only an electrical fire," Chuck called out on the radio. "There's nothing else in the cockpit to burn."

There was a moment of silence and then we heard Ridley's indignant voice: "What do you mean, nothing else? I'm in here."

On another X-1 flight Chuck Yeager got into trouble at altitude and accidentally exclaimed over the radio: "Oh, my God!"

The radio was silent for a long moment and then a deep voice came on the air: "Yes, my son?" Everyone was startled at first, especially Chuck, but it broke the tension.

I was flying chase plane and Chuck has always accused me

of answering him. However, I think it was Jack Russell, the X-1 crew chief, who was listening in on the ground.

On August 25 I took the X-1 up on my seventh flight for another attempt to reach maximum altitude above 73,000 feet. Preparation and take-off were normal and the climb to drop altitude was routine. At 7,000 feet I left the bomb bay of the B-29 and went down on the little aluminum elevator into the cockpit of the X-1. Jack Ridley came down behind me with the door and helped me slide it into place, It was after he had gone back into the bomber and I was looking around the cockpit that I first saw a small crack in the canopy along the edge.

It was a tiny break only an inch long, and as it appeared to be confined to the inner shell of the plexiglas canopy, I did not feel it important enough to call off the flight. Remembering all the time, money, and hard work that had gone into preparations for my flight and the many people who were depending upon me to make it successful, I did not want to seem overly cautious. I watched the crack but it didn't get any larger, and as we neared the drop I had almost forgotten about it.

The drop and rocket start were clean and quick. Chuck Yeager and Kit Murray were behind me in F-80 chase planes and confirmed that my engine was going. With three chambers burning I pointed the nose of the X-1 skyward and once more felt the tremendous surge of power thrusting the little airplane into the heavens. In seconds I passed through the buffet region, leveled off and went supersonic, then pulled up again and continued my climb.

Suddenly I heard a loud "poof" in the cockpit and my pressure suit inflated almost instantaneously. In a flash I realized that I had lost my cockpit pressure. Glancing up at the canopy, I saw with a start that the one-inch crack had extended back six or eight inches, then turned left and broken completely through. The life-saving pressure in which I was immersed in the sealed cockpit had now vanished into the pitiless sky.

Momentarily stunned, I hesitated for a fraction of a second. Altitude was 65,000 feet. I was acutely aware that the low pressure in rarified air at this altitude would boil my blood like water if my pressure suit failed. Then moving abruptly to regain command of the situation, I cut my engine and in the same motion shoved the control wheel all the way forward and nosed over sharply in a steep dive.

Watching my vapor trail high above them, my chase pilots could see that my rockets had stopped burning, and Chuck Yeager came on the air in a worried voice to ask if anything was wrong.

I was unable to reply coherently. The viselike pressure suit, constricting my body and limbs in its lifesaving grip, made breathing difficult and talking well-nigh impossible. In any event, my whole attention now centered on returning to a safe altitude while I was still conscious and able to command the airplane. My only reply to Chuck was a series of grunts that were not only incomprehensible but no doubt alarming.

These garbled sounds, coming over the radio, only served to increase his agitation. Again he came on the air, and again I tried in vain to answer. Now the diving airplane was at 30,000 feet, under control but still supersonic, and as the denser air took hold of the control surfaces I pulled back on the wheel and began to guide the X-1 toward level flight.

At 20,000 feet, in human air once more and breathing normally again, I relaxed for the first time. With my left hand I opened the valve that dumped the pressure in my suit. As the viselike grip relaxed I took a deep breath of relief and felt the tension begin to flow out of my arms and legs.

"Everything's O.K.," I called over the radio. "The canopy broke and I had to come down in a hurry." I was sobered by the realization that the untried pressure suit was the only thing that had saved my life.

I could hear Chuck's low exclamation as he realized what had happened, but he said nothing more. Then I dumped the remaining propellants in my fuel tanks, and with the F-80's flying very close to me now, I began the familiar circle and descent toward the lake bed and home.

While waiting for a new canopy to be built and shipped to Muroc, the decision was made by Bell and the Air Force to discontinue the high-altitude program for the time being. As the result of my experience to date, they felt that even a perfect flight under optimum conditions would yield only another two or three thousand feet. As this would not have any significant value over what had already been accomplished, they decided that the cost of additional altitude tests was not justified. Of course, improved models of the X-1 were built and flown later and set new speed and altitude records.

We continued routine tests in the original airplane, checking out more pilots in rocket flying to give us a cadre of experienced men we could fall back on when the later planes were ready. I made a total of ten flights in the first X-1, giving me the most rocket experience next to Yeager. It was just as well, as the time was coming when I would need all the experience I could get.

The original X-1 was subsequently retired from service and now occupies a place of honor in the famous Smithsonian Institution in Washington. With the altitude program completed, I returned to Wright Field in September to resume jet testing, and in April, 1950, transferred permanently to Muroc.

7

Edwards

The western Mojave Desert is a land of naked mountains, sandstorms, and Joshua trees. Death Valley lies due north. In this barren waste, where the total rainfall is only 4 inches a year, summer temperatures average 100 degrees—in the shade. A sirocco wind blows continually from the west. Lifeless in the center of this wasteland lies Rogers Dry Lake, 65 square miles of fine clay and silt. When dried out, it cracks. When dug up, it looks and feels like face powder—neutral shade. In the winter when the rains come, water drains from the surrounding mountains and covers the lake. Then the wind blows it back and forth, filling the cracks and smoothing over the ground. Two months later, when the rain ends, the water evaporates. Then for ten months the lake is dry again.

Perfectly flat, 15 miles across and strong enough to support the heaviest aircraft without breaking, the Rogers Dry Lake bed is the world's finest natural airfield. Except in the rainy season, skies are always clear, and ceiling and visibility are above flying minimums 350 days a year. Towns—and people—are few. The surrounding mountains and miles of desert discourage visitors. Yet the population centers of Southern California are only two hours away. Metropolitan Los Angeles lies 100 miles southwest. So do most of America's major aircraft factories—Douglas at Santa Monica, Lockheed at Burbank, North American at Inglewood, and Northrop at Hawthorne. Convair at San Diego is not much farther.

Commercial pilots and private flyers, recognizing the advantages of the secluded dry lake for test flying, have lifted new planes off this natural landing field since aircraft manufacturing first began in Southern California. In World War II the Army Air Corps also realized its value. After Pearl Harbor a 650-foot model of a Japanese cruiser, erected at the south end of the deserted lake, made a life-size bomb target for student pilots. In 1942, the north end of the lake, still more secluded, became the secret test field for the Bell P-59, America's first jet-powered airplane. Most of the nation's new military planes have been tested here ever since.

When war ended, the flight test base on the north and the training base on the south were merged in a single flight test center, set up by the new U.S. Air Force to conduct experimental engineering and test flying. Remote, safe, and secure, it offered ideal take-off and landing conditions for the high-speed jet and rocket planes of the postwar era. With miles of natural landing field, where even a crippled aircraft could land in comparative safety, new and experimental planes could take to the air with a reasonable chance of getting back down.

Edwards was first known as Muroc Air Force Base, named for the Corum brothers who homesteaded the area years before. In the airpower cutback after World War II, when flying funds were slashed and no money was available for new building, life at Muroc strongly resembled pioneer days. Barracks and mess halls were wartime wooden shacks covered with peeling tar paper. Family housing for military dependents was nonexistent. In this borax and alkali desert, experimental pilots flew the first rocket planes beyond the sound barrier and tested the new jet fighters and bombers of America's postwar Air Force. Then after five years of neglect, war in Korea turned the nation's eyes skyward and flying funds were forthcoming again. As Congress belatedly voted new billions for air defenses, the Air Force Flight Test Center at Rogers Dry Lake began to expand.

Renamed Edwards Air Force Base in honor of Captain Glen W. Edwards, a test pilot killed in a crash of the experimental B-49 "Flying Wing" bomber, a modern flying laboratory took shape in the California desert. Under General Albert Boyd, commanding officer who brought it west from Wright Field, the new test center became the second largest Air Force installation in the country. On this site of nearly

300,000 acres, four government agencies and a score of manufacturers established permanent organizations. Test facilities mushroomed. A new rocket engine test stand was built for static testing in the remote recesses of Leuhman Ridge. A high-speed track, the world's fastest railway, provided ground tests of aircraft and pilots at speeds up to 1,500 miles an hour. An enlarged test pilot school offered instruction to military and civilian students from the U.S. and foreign countries. An all-altitude speed course and a space-positioning range were developed to aid in testing new and experimental planes, and a new precision bombing range was created to develop aerial bombs and their components.

Early in 1951, under the impact of technological progress, the Air Force divorced aircraft design from its procurement services and the new Air Research and Development Command was set up with Edwards as one of the first four test centers (today there are ten). As activity increased at Edwards, so did its population. To meet the shortage of rental housing in nearby Lancaster, Mojave, Palmdale, Rosamond,

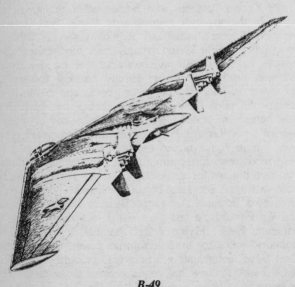

B-49

and Boron, the town of Edwards was expanded with 1,350 new family housing units. To supplement the service commissary, Post Exchange, and filling station on the base, a modern shopping center was built at Edwards complete with supermarket, beauty parlor, drugstore, and restaurants. An influx of married personnel and civilian workers brought families with children. To educate them a new elementary school with 850 desks and a Desert High School with 250 desks were added.

On the base new construction improved existing facilities for aircraft maintenance and flying operations. The Santa Fe Railroad track, which ran diagonally across Rogers Dry Lake, was moved north and the roadbed was resurfaced. The world's longest concrete runway, 15,000 feet in length, was built adjoining the lake bed for new and bigger planes and for rainy season service. Funds were provided for a new headquarters building, bachelor quarters, and cafeteria on the base. Existing aircraft hangars were moved 2 miles across the desert to a new maintenance area that included a third hangar, a new maintenance and modification hangar, and a jet engine repair and overhaul facility. Manufacturers also enlarged their own test facilities.

Today Edwards is a modern small city of 10,000, including 6,500 civilians employed by Civil Service and contractors.

The rocket engine test laboratory on the sides of Leuhman Ridge provides facilities for static testing of high-thrust engines. Control rooms and observation points for scientists and engineers are located in reinforced concrete blockhouses, where civilian contractors and Air Force personnel work together to solve complex problems of testing and firing high-speed rockets for missiles and aircraft.

The all-altitude speed course provides accurate determination of speed at any altitude. It consists of three radio beams forming planes perpendicular to the line of flight that activate electronic timing devices for accurate measurement of ultrasonic speeds. Another new facility is the high-precision space-positioning range, which provides precise trajectory data for experimental and prototype aircraft. It was designed to give a mean deviation of only 5 feet in measurement of aircraft positions throughout an area 125 miles long, 45 miles wide, and 35 miles high. This facility was developed to answer two primary questions: in an experimental aircraft, what was it able to accomplish in performance? and in a prototype aircraft, did it meet its specifications?

The precision bombing range at Edwards researches and develops experimental and standard aerial bombs and components. Optical and electronic instruments designed and built expressly for the range obtain space measurements accurate to .01 of 1 per cent and time measurements to .001 seconds. Data obtained from test runs on this range are used in compiling Air Force bombing tables.

Upon reporting to Edwards in April, 1950, I was assigned to the flight test section as assistant chief. In those days it was a small organization of seven pilots, headed by Major Gust Askounis, a former Wright Field associate. Other pilots were Captain Jack Ridley, the X-1 engineer; Captain Kit Murray, who later established a new altitude record in the X-1; Captain Charles Yeager, first man to fly faster than sound; Captain Wilbur Sellers, who later was killed flying an F-94 jet fighter; and Lt. James Nash.

This was a very happy occasion for me. I had been trying to get out to Edwards permanently ever since my temporary assignment in 1949, for I realized that it was destined to become the headquarters for test flying. New planes were on the drawing boards and under construction that would be flown at Edwards and this was an opportunity to get in on the ground floor. They would be flown by Edwards test pilots and I hoped to participate.

Our test program consisted of seven parts or phases, with the manufacturer of the airplane responsible for Phases 1 and 3 and the Air Force conducting the remainder. Of these, three were performed by Edwards test pilots, who also participated actively, with the manufacturer, in Phases 1 and 3.

After the manufacturer had flown the prototype airplane to see if it met specifications, we took it over for Phase 2 testing. We checked the manufacturer's performance figures, made sure the plane met contract requirements, determined its handling characteristics, and evaluated its potential value. This required constant observation and precision flying. We had a six-day week and work often started at 4 A.M. Needless to say, it called for a real love of flying.

Upon completing Phase 2 tests, we returned the airplane to the manufacturer to make any changes we felt were needed. This covered the whole range from engine performance to the control system and air-frame design. When we were satisfied that the deficiencies had been overcome, we took the plane back once more for Phase 4 testing. This is devoted to detailed performance flying, plus stability and control checks in detail. Performance data are compiled and checked against the manufacturer's own figures. They also go into the pilot's handbook for use when the airplane enters squadron service.

New models that passed these tests went back to the Wright Air Development Center at Dayton, Ohio, for all-weather testing. Upon completion they returned to Edwards for Phase 6 tests in accelerated service, intended to gather full operational data on production models in the shortest possible time. Compressing normal flying into a few short weeks, we would fly several airplanes around the clock, if necessary, to compile complete operating information. Phase 7, a continuation of Phase 6 tests, is conducted by the Air Proving Ground and using commands to determine performance under simulated combat conditions and in squadron service. Only after a new plane has successfully passed all these tests is it acceptable for service in the Air Force.

Despite the many long hours we spent in the air, flying was only a small part of flight testing. It was the most important part, naturally, but unless we turned in a good, precise, and understandable report of the test, its usefulness was limited to the air base where we operated. The project officers at ARDC and AMC and the project people at Air Force headquarters in Washington also needed to know the problems of the new planes we were testing. For this reason we spent many long hours writing our reports, computing the flight data, and making certain that all information we put down was clear and complete.

It was not enough to say that an airplane wasn't very good: we had to give our reasons and recommend changes to correct the problem. I spent many hours writing and dictating reports, and later on when I became chief of flight test, the hardest part of my job was keeping on the pilots and making sure the reports were in on time. As they all came over my desk, of course I was responsible. I also had to make sure the pilots were giving the right answers, so I went out and flew the airplanes they were testing to be sure I understood the problems.

With the advent of the Korean War in June, 1950, we began getting bad news about the performance of our jet fighters in combat. Lockheed F-80's and later Republic F-84's went into action as fighter bombers against ground targets and the first reports weren't too good. Many people claimed that the jet was too fast to hit ground targets, couldn't carry enough bombs and rockets, and burned fuel too fast to be effective at low altitudes. Many Air Force commanders reported that the old propeller-driven fighter bombers from World War II days were doing a better job.

This was understandable to us at Edwards. We recognized the deficiencies of the early jets against ground targets, due to their limited armament and range. But we also noted that our pilots had not met enemy air opposition, and at such time as it appeared, we suggested they would be quite glad to have the jets. Jet speed would then become an advantage in overtaking and destroying enemy aircraft, and also in defending our own ground forces against air attack.

As the first reports of jet shortcomings came back from the field commanders, we began flight tests at Edwards on three new planes that seemed made to order for ground support. They were a new kind of jet called a penetration fighter, designed for long-range operations, maximum endurance over the target, and ability to inflict and absorb lots of punishment down low in range of ground fire. Ordered three years earlier in an Air Force design competition, prototype airplanes had been built and flown by the manufacturers, and now we began our own tests to evaluate their performance.

These planes were the McDonnell F-88, the Lockheed F-90, and the North American F-93. The 88 was a twin-engined jet, big and powerful, and the forerunner of the supersonic McDonnell F-101 that appeared in 1954. Its higher performance, good maneuverability, and ease of handling made it our first choice. The F-90 was a heavy airplane with high wing-loading, which limited its maneuverability. It was strongly built and we felt it would be hard to shoot down, but it lacked the performance to do any fighting against other planes.

The F-93 was a beefed-up F-86. North American had installed afterburning to increase its performance, which limited its effectiveness as a penetration fighter, since it would burn fuel too fast to go very far. The F-88 won the design competition. We were very enthusiastic about its potential and recommended it for procurement. At that time, however, McDonnell was fully occupied on Navy contracts and had no place to build the airplane. As a result, the Air Force decided not to build any of the three.

As a substitute, we ordered two new models of the F-86 Sabre Jet, the E and F. With a bigger engine, they had more speed and could carry a 2,000-pound bomb load over 500 miles and return. The F model, designed for use as either a fighter or fighter-bomber, made its first flight in March, 1952. This plane did not completely fill the requirement for a penetration fighter, but it was ordered into production anyway, and together with the sweptwing F-84F, which was developed about the same time, it was used until better planes came along.

I flew performance and stability tests on the E model, the first plane ever built with a so-called "flying tail." The elevator and stabilizer, built as a single movable surface, offered a great improvement over earlier models, whose fixed tail surfaces restricted their maneuverability at high speeds.

Coupled with the movable tail was the first completely irreversible hydraulic control system ever designed in a production aircraft. With this system there was no longer any danger of control surfaces reversing themselves at high speeds, as we had experienced in supersonic dives in earlier jets. It did present a new problem, however, because it decreased the pilot's feel of the airplane. Now he operated hydraulic valves instead of stick forces, and the valves operated the controls. This raised the possibility that he might overcontrol the airplane and damage it in violent maneuvers. But after we installed artificial "feel" devices to aid him, we were quite happy with the new system and recommended that it be used in the future on all new jets.

During my first years at Edwards the famous woman aviator, Jacqueline Cochran, began visiting the base to familiarize herself with jet aircraft. An Air Force reserve lieutenant colonel, she had permission from Air Force headquarters to be checked out in jets. Chuck Yeager worked with her most of the time, giving her dual instruction in a Lockheed T-33 jet trainer, and later checked her out in an F-86. She established a world's speed record for women in a Canadian-built 86 with a Canadian engine, and also became the first woman to attain supersonic speed, which she accomplished in a dive over Edwards in an 86. In my opinion, she is a very unusual woman, having the desire to participate in dangerous flights in high-speed jet aircraft. She is an outstanding flyer and I consider her a very close friend, as I do her husband, Floyd Odlum.

In August, 1951, Lt. Col. Askounis moved up to a new assignment as chief of staff for maintenance and materiel and I replaced him as chief of flight test operations, a job I held for the next five years. Life had been fun before, but now as so-called chief test pilot for the Air Force, I settled down and became serious. New responsibilities made me a changed man.

In sixteen months the flight test operations division had nearly tripled in size. We now had twenty pilots, compared to seven when I came to Edwards, and maintenance and house-keeping personnel had increased correspondingly. To operate the division more efficiently and also to free myself for more flying, I reorganized the division into three branches. I named branch chiefs to supervise the respective test programs on fighters, bombers, and cargo planes and helicopters. Together with Captain Sellers, my assistant, they relieved me of details and paper work, permitting me to devote most of my time to actual flying.

Colonel Boyd, now a brigadier general, continued to participate with us in flying all the new planes. He was always a pilot's pilot and we had a great deal of respect and affection for him. Major Yeager and I had become very close to him, in fact, and regarded him almost as a relative. In many ways he was like a father to us—an Air Force father. We also felt a close kinship to General Earl Partridge, who had come back from Korea to head up the new ARDC. On visits to Edwards he took every opportunity to fly the latest planes and made a point of talking to the test pilots and getting our firsthand opinion on the planes we were flying. I still retain my high regard for General Partridge, who at this writing is commander of the Continental Air Defense Command.

I remember checking him out in the Boeing B-47 at Edwards on one of his frequent visits to our base. This is a six-jet medium bomber designed and built soon after World War II. Weighing over 200,000 pounds, it carries a bomb load of 10 tons more than 3,000 miles at speeds over 600 miles an hour. Named the Stratojet, it is the fastest medium bomber in the world. On his first flight in this airplane Gen. Partridge flew it as if he had many hours in it.

I also flew many hours in the B-47, conducting Phase 4 tests for performance and stability, and also running bomb tests at various speeds and altitudes. The information thus compiled became the basis for bombing tables for use by bombardiers when they flew training missions later in this airplane.

Col. Guy Townsend, the project test pilot, checked me out in the B-52 intercontinental bomber at the main Boeing plant

B-47

in Seattle. Named the Stratofortress, it weighs 350,000 pounds, can fly at altitudes over 50,000 feet and has a top speed over 650 miles an hour. Its eight J-57 engines develop a total thrust of 80,000 pounds. Range and bomb load are classified information, but it has flown nonstop around the world using in-flight refueling. Today it is the principal weapon in the Strategic Air Command.

My first flights in the B-52 were made at Moses Lake, an airfield east of Seattle where the giant bomber had more room to get off the ground. It is a very large airplane, nearly fifty feet high and with wings almost 200 feet from end to end. When I taxied out for take-off the outboard riggers on the wing-tips extended over on the dirt beside the taxi strip. Despite its great size, however, the B-52 took off and climbed rapidly. I made several manuevers at altitude and then made a speed run. Performance was comparable to the F-86 jet fighter's, if not a bit faster, and I noticed that our 86 chase plane had trouble keeping up with us. The bomber's control system is very responsive, and for all its size, I found I could maneuver it like a fighter plane.

Like the B-47, however, it is hard to slow down; when something that heavy gets going fast, its clean aerodynamic design offers little air resistance, even with power off. This was especially a problem on the B-47 during final approach and landing. However, with the use of dive brakes on the B-52, which also improve lateral control, the pilot can maintain any approach speed he needs. All in all, it is a very pleasant airplane to fly, and today is the first-line bomber in the Air Force.

The first B-52's were built with seating tandem like the B-47, with the copilot sitting behind the pilot under one canopy. In later models, however, the copilot was moved up beside the pilot to give him visual observation of fuel manipulation and sequencing. I personally had the opinion that they should have been left in tandem. Visibility was better, as both pilots had unobstructed vision on both sides and behind. The B-52 today does not have the excellent visibility provided in the early airplanes.

As a side light on this point, I feel that today's commercial airliners and the new jet transports on order also have inferior visibility for the same reasons. In my opinion the pilot should be put up in a bubble canopy as in the B-47 cockpit. If this had been done earlier, perhaps some mid-air collisions such as the Bryce Canyon disaster where two airliners ran together could have been prevented. It is certainly something to think about for the future when the skies will become more and more crowded. All the traffic control in the world will not prevent collisions, but better visibility will greatly reduce the chance of accidents.

A year after I went to Edwards, the Air Research and Development Command was created. It grew out of the realization in all top echelons of the Air Force that design and testing of new planes could no longer be handled properly by the Air Materiel Command. With the best intentions in the world, AMC project officers found it impossible to combine development and procurement. Often aware that a new plane had deficiencies that should be corrected before it was built, they were also under pressure to get it into production. Many times they were forced to do so despite their better judgment. The result was that on many occasions new aircraft had to be returned to the manufacturer for expensive modification programs after they had been delivered and accepted by tactical organizations.

With the creation of ARDC, we were better able to get the bugs out of a new plane before it went into mass production. The test pilot could say "no" until he was satisfied that it met its specifications. He was not under the same pressures to produce airplanes in ARDC, which is not responsible for procurement. By the same token, the AMC project officer was relieved of the responsibility for technical decisions. He was no longer required to decide whether to continue production, slow it down, or not begin at all. These decisions were taken off his shoulders. Now he needed only to wait until ARDC told him the airplane was satisfactory; we gave him the O.K. signal that told him it was ready to buy.

With the creation of ARDC also came the new weapons system concept—the joint development of an airframe, power plant, and armament as a single unit for production. It made certain that the hundreds of accessory items of government-furnished equipment were built to the same specifications. All too often in the past, the airframe manufacturer had found himself with pieces that did not fit together. Project officers worked separately on each item—for example, the engine, the guns, and the gunsight. Each was a separate project and was procured independently for installation in the completed airplane. Everybody was a specialist, but all too often the finished parts didn't match up.

For example, improved engine models grew in size and didn't fit in the fuselage—because only the engine project officer knew it was bigger. Similarly, an airplane's armament might be changed without corresponding modification of the firing mechanism—again because no one else knew about it. The resulting delay and confusion as we struggled to correct these errors were always costly and time-consuming.

Under the new weapons system concept, a task-force group of project officers has common responsibility for the complete airplane. These officers work at adjoining desks from the same set of master plans and share progress reports on all aircraft components. Design changes are jointly agreed upon with full provision for any resulting modifications. In this way today's complex airplane progresses intelligently from blueprint to finished hardware as a planned package ready for the assembly line.

In 1952 General Boyd received a new command assignment in ARDC and prepared to leave Edwards. I was very sorry to see him go but wished him the best of luck and success. He told me to let him know if I ever wanted to work for him again, as he would be more than happy to have me back in his command. On several occasions I have thought about taking him up on his offer, not only because I think he is an outstanding officer, but because every man likes to work for people he admires and respects.

However, my primary interest was in flight testing, and so I remained at Edwards. But after working with General Boyd more than six years, there was a nostalgic feeling when he left Edwards. He was part of the inspiration for all of us, and when he was gone a lot of it departed with him. To me he was an ideal, after whom I had patterned myself and my thoughts and efforts in flight testing.

General Boyd was replaced by Brig. Gen. J. S. Holtoner, under whom I served the next four years. He was a capable administrator and under his leadership the Edwards Flight

Test Center continued to grow. Colonel Horace Hanes, the new director of flight test, became my immediate superior, replacing Colonel F. J. Ascani. Working under their supervision, we flew and tested the greatest number of new types and models of aircraft in the history of our country.

These included the new Century series of supersonic jet fighters from the F-100 to the new F-105; the B-52 and B-58 jet bombers; new transports like the turboprop C-130 and the jet KC-135; and the experimental rocket ships, the Bell X-1 and the unknown X-2. With production models of planes we flew and tested during this period, America completed its transition to history's first all-jet Air Force.

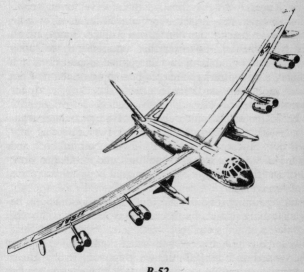

B-52

8

Jet Force

War in Korea, with the constant threat of an even greater conflict, brought new urgency to the need for an all-weather jet fighter to defend the continental United States against attack from the air. To meet this requirement, we turned initially to early models of two jet combat aircraft already in existence, which offered at least a beginning on the new and pressing problem of air defense.

The first of these planes was the Lockheed F-94 Starfire, adapted by the manufacturer from the T-33 jet trainer, which was a two-seat version of the familiar F-80 Shooting Star. Armed with 50-caliber machine guns and equipped with nose radar for all-weather search capabilities, the F-94A had flown in 1948 and the prototype of an improved B model was tested the following year.

About the same time the Northrop Aircraft Company, designer and builder of night fighters in World War II, brought out a two-seat jet interceptor with all-weather capabilities. This was the F-89 Scorpion, which also made its first flight in 1948. Armed with six 20-millimeter cannon, it had greater fire power than the 94, and as it was a bigger airplane with more fuel capacity, it offered comparable speed with more range. Both of these aircraft were in the 600-mph class and could fly above 45,000 feet. In addition, both carried a two-man crew, with a radar operator in addition to the pilot to operate the early radar equipment of that time.

The F-94 was the first to go into production and become operational, followed closely by new models of both the F-89 and F-94. These included new rocket-armed models with bigger engines, giving higher speeds and greater fire power, which substantially increased the nation's air defenses. The Lockheed F-94C, first fighter plane ever built without guns or cannon, was armed with two dozen air-to-air rockets mounted in a ring around its radar nose. Both the 94C and Northrop's D model of the F-89 which followed it carried additional rockets on the wings.

The early models of both these airplanes, in my opinion, did not have the speed or fire power needed to intercept enemy jet bombers. The 94C offered higher performance but was quite controversial. Lockheed had invested its own money in this airplane and of course was desirous of building it for the Air Force. However, we at the Edwards Flight Test Center felt that the cost of putting it into production was not worth the slight amount of increased performance it offered.

North American Aviation got in the all-weather sweep-stakes late but finished out in front. Its entry was the F-86D, an all-weather version of the famed Sabre Jet, which at the time was our fastest and best jet fighter. The 86D was the second all-rocket interceptor to be built for air defense duty, carrying twenty-four Mighty Mouse rockets as its sole armament. A sweptwing airplane of superior design, it was much faster than the other all-weather jets, with a top speed over 700 miles an hour. With this kind of speed and comparable altitude and range, it obviously offered better protection against enemy attack by high-speed jet bombers. Unlike the other all-weather jets, however, it was a one-man airplane, with the pilot operating the radar.

For this reason the 86D was also a controversial airplane. It was widely felt at the time that one man could not fly the airplane and also operate the radar. We ran many tests and evaluations to determine if it could be done. The upshot was that both the pilot and the equipment proved to be adequate for the mission and the 86D was ordered into production. It gave us the higher-performance airplane we needed. I was of the opinion, as were many other pilots, that we should have concentrated on the 86D in lieu of F-89's and F-94's, because performancewise it was a much better airplane.

The introduction of air-to-air rockets as armament on jet interceptors at this time also changed the tactics of aerial interception. With the cannon and machine guns on the early F-89's and F-94's you still had to overtake and attack the target from the rear in an old-fashioned fighter-pursuit intercept. As a result, in an instrument attack with radar you were prone to run up the bomber's tail, especially under conditions of zero visibility in darkness and bad weather. Now with air-to-air rockets we were able to make a 90-degree intercept, flying a lead collision course. The radar would compute the intercept and at a certain time the rockets would fire automatically. Then you would get the pull-out signal and maneuver away in time to avoid colliding with the airplane you were intercepting. This is an easier and safer method, because you can fire your rockets away from the intruder's line of flight, and you are not subjected to fire from his tail guns.

Despite all these improvements, however, we still needed a faster airplane, which we got in the 86D. Of course, it was an interim airplane to fill the gap until the Convair F-102 came into service. This would be a supersonic all-weather fighter with improved radar and armed with the Hughes Falcon guided missile. It is now in production and is taking its place as our first-line air defense interceptor. With this airplane we can overtake and destroy any known enemy bomber day or night in any kind of weather.

The 102 is a big delta-wing airplane which was developed from the early XF-92, a research plane built to determine whether a delta-design was feasible. This was the first delta-wing aircraft built and flown anywhere, and provided much useful information on the delta design. It was also the first delta platform ever to achieve supersonic flight.

To reach supersonic speed in this airplane you had to attain a very steep dive angle and it would just barely get through the sound barrier. It simply lacked power to go any faster. However, we found that the delta platform handled very well during the transition from subsonic to supersonic speeds, in comparison with the straight-wing F-94 and the sweptwing F-86, which encountered severe buffeting and loss of control effectiveness in this speed region. These problems did not exist in the F-92, which gave us a pretty good idea that the delta platform would handle very well in supersonic flight. It also had a lower wing loading, which enabled it to fly higher.

*   *   *

The F-102 was typical of a whole new breed of airplanes, the Century series, which were designed and built in the months and years following the outbreak of the Korean War. They represented a tremendous advance in aircraft design and development. The first production airplanes in this country capable of supersonic speed in level flight, they embodied widely differing design philosophies, yet each was successful and proved to be an outstanding vehicle for its mission. In fifteen short months from May, 1953, to September, 1954, no less than four new Century series fighters made their first flights. Among them were two new day fighters, a long-range escort fighter, and an all-weather interceptor. They included sweptwing, delta wing, and straight-wing designs. All are the best aircraft of their type in this country, and undoubtedly the best in the world.

Soon after the North American F-100, the first in the new Century series, began its flight test program in May, 1953, Convair brought the first F-102 to Edwards for Phase 1 testing. The pilot was my good friend, Dick Johnson, who had resigned from the Air Force to become chief pilot on the 102 for Convair. I escorted him on the early flights when he encountered several stability and control problems. After delays required to work them out, we took the 102 up again and attempted to get it supersonic straight and level. To our surprise and concern, the airplane would not reach Mach 1.

This was a keen disappointment to the Air Force and the Air Defense Command, which had been counting heavily on the 102 for a badly-needed supersonic all-weather fighter. The failure of the new delta-wing interceptor to attain its design speed was a serious blow to us, as well as to the manufacturer. Production was halted while the Air Force took another look at the whole 102 program. The National Advisory Committee for Aeronautics, which participated in the early design studies, had claimed all along that the airplane would not go supersonic, and now their predictions had come true. If the 102 could not offer much better performance than the F-86D, which it was intended to replace, there was no justification for going ahead with the program.

Fortunately for all concerned, the 102 was saved by a redesigned fuselage based on wind-tunnel studies of Richard

Whitcomb, an aeronautical engineer for NACA. He had discovered that an airplane with a pinched waist at the wing roots would go faster because it offered less air resistance. This was especially true of the 102, which encountered excessive drag rise because of the bulk of its big triangular wings. After many tests Convair applied the Whitcomb theory and other modifications to the 102 to reduce drag. The airplane slipped easily past the sound barrier and kept right on going. Today it is a fine supersonic all-weather fighter, the best in the world.

The next in the Century series to fly, the Lockheed F-104, made its first flight at Edwards in February, 1954. I flew it for the first time the following August. A day fighter in its original configuration, it is an air superiority weapon designed to sweep the skies of enemy planes. In comparison with other fighter planes at that time, which were quite heavy and weighed from 25,000 to 40,000 pounds, the 104 is a lightweight airplane, with a design weight of only 16,000 pounds.

The prototype airplane did not offer a large increase in performance over our other new planes; powered by a Curtiss-Wright J-65 jet engine until the newer General Electric J-79 was available, the first 104 was not capable of reaching its maximum performance. However, even with a smaller engine, our preliminary evaluation flights indicated that it was a very nice airplane to fly. It had one of the best, if not the best, flight control systems of any of the 100-series airplanes. We were most happy with the flight control system and told other manufacturers that if they would use it they would have much better planes.

With the advent of the 104, we found ourselves with a production airplane capable of going beyond Mach 2. Fortunately, the increased performance was not enough to create control problems. Both the F-100 and F-101 were capable of speeds above Mach 1.5, or one and a half times the speed of sound, so we had precedents for its operation.

Of course, the later 100-series airplanes, with their blazing speeds, did create a new tactical problem. We could not take take these airplanes to high altitudes and stay there very long. They lost considerable thrust in the rarified air above 50,000 feet and consequently could not maintain altitude. However,

F-100

their speed itself enabled us to overcome this problem. With the speed we could gain in level flight at lower altitudes, we could zoom up to the stratosphere on sheer momentum. Once at maximum altitude, these planes can stay long enough to accomplish their mission and destroy any enemy intruder.

Last in the Century series to fly was the McDonnell F-101, the successor to the F-88 penetration fighter we'd liked so much when we evaluated the earlier airplane four years before. A bigger, more powerful airplane, equipped with two J-57 engines, the 101 was built to be a long-range escort or an interdiction fighter; it can play either role. As a fighter-bomber it can carry the atom bomb; or replace the bombs with external fuel tanks and it can be used for long-range escort work.

Possessing excellent design and lots of power, the 101 proved to be very fast. With the large amount of thrust available we experienced an entirely new area of rapid acceleration. It would climb to altitude very rapidly and also had a very high Mach number. We had several pilots who lost their landing gear doors on take-off because they exceeded the gear limit air speed of 250 knots before they could get their wheels up. Speed was comparable to the first Lockheed F-104, which came out a few months earlier, and next to the 104 it is the fastest plane in the Air Force.

We encountered a pitch-up in the 101, or a tendency of the plane to nose up in the air suddenly. We are hoping to overcome it by installing a "stick-snatcher," which will automatically compensate for pitchup by causing the pilot to release back pressure on the control stick when maneuvering. We have lost a few airplanes because of this condition; if the angle of attack becomes critical before the pilot can correct it he loses control.

With the advent of the F-101 and F-104 we found that a new armament system was needed to take advantage of their increased speed. Today's supersonic fighter plane, closing with an enemy at several times the speed of sound, is in firing range of the target for only brief seconds, then is miles away again. What was needed was a higher rate of fire than the air-to-air rocket and machine gun. What we got was the T-61 Gatling cannon, a weapon with more fire power than had ever been experienced. Designed and developed for the F-104, the new Gatling cannon is the fastest gun in the world. Despite its blazing speed, the 104 can throw a lot of lead at the target, thus increasing its kill potential considerably. The F-101, which also gets in and out very fast, has been armed with improved conventional cannon and guided missiles.

We also found that both airplanes flew so fast that the pilot did not have enough time to set up his firing pass after he spotted a target. Human vision simply could not see far enough ahead. To give him more time for target identification we equipped both planes with a search-radar installation that enabled him to look well beyond his normal field of vision. With its help he searches the skies and can identify enemy planes in time to attack them before he is miles on the other side.

As a result of Air Force interest in procuring the best combat aircraft, and through cooperation of the Navy and its manufacturers, we tested many of the Navy's new jet aircraft for evaluation and comparison. In the years after Korea, as money for improved designs became available, several advanced types of shipboard fighters were produced and flown. Of those which we tested, the Chance-Vought F7U Cutlass, the Douglas F4D Skyray, the McDonnell F3H Demon, the North American FJ3 Fury, and the new Chance-Vought F8U Crusader were outstanding.

The Chance-Vought Cutlass was a medium-weight fighter powered by a Westinghouse J-46 engine producing 8,200 pounds of thrust with afterburner. It had a service ceiling of 45,000 feet and a top speed over 650 miles an hour. We found that it handled well, but performancewise it wasn't too much faster than our own F-86 Sabre Jet. For this reason we recommended that it be dropped from consideration.

When we tested the Douglas F4D Skyray, we found that it handled very much like a trainer. Low-altitude performance was excellent, but it did not perform so well at higher altitudes where the airplane would normally be fighting. It had other serious problems, which apparently were difficult to overcome, as it was a long time getting into service. We thought the airplane had a good potential, but it has never lived up to our expectations, and today I consider its performance unacceptable.

The McDonnell Demon was an all-weather high-performance interceptor with speed over 600 miles an hour. A big airplane, it had the armament and range to handle fighter-bomber missions. However, like the North American Fury, the Navy version of the F-86, we felt it had limited performance and was not worthy of Air Force procurement. On the other hand, the new Chance-Vought Crusader was an excellent airplane. A supersonic day fighter able to carry missiles as well as conventional armament, it is today the best fighter plane the Navy has in service.

We recommended that it be watched closely and if it developed as anticipated, the Air Force would do well to consider it as a possible addition to our Century series fighters. When we evaluated the F8U it lacked good aileron control at high Mach numbers, but as it is being accepted for tactical use, apparently this deficiency has been corrected. In this airplane the Navy has a fighter that is capable of having the same performance as our fighters, and I would estimate its performance is very close to that of our own F-101.

I also got a chance to fly the Navy's Skyrocket, a swept-wing research plane built by Douglas Aircraft Company in both jet and rocket-engine versions. Gene Mays flew it first and then Bill Bridgeman of Douglas took it to new speed and altitude records. I did a lot of escort chasing for them and later for Scotty Crossfield, the NACA pilot, and Colonel Marion Carl, the famous Marine test pilot. The airplane interested us because it was able to go to high speeds and altitudes, and I personally wanted to fly it to get firsthand information on a sweptwing rocket plane at high Mach numbers.

My first ride was in the jet-rocket combination airplane that had limited performance, and was little more than a familiarization flight. Later I flew the straight-rocket D-558-2 to Mach 1.5 and an altitude around 65,000 feet. This was quite an experience, as the airplane did not handle too well at high speeds. However, it had good visibility and a comfortable cockpit, and it did give me some firsthand experience in a sweptwing rocket plane above Mach 1, which perhaps helped me later on with the X-2 program.

After Bill Bridgeman completed flight tests on the Skyrocket, he began testing a newer Douglas research plane, designed to investigate supersonic flight with a turbojet engine. This was the straight-wing X-3, which I was the second pilot to fly. After Bridgeman had completed the preliminary tests but before Douglas turned it over to the National Advisory Committee for Aeronautics, the Air Force requested permission to evaluate its flight characteristics and performance. As a result, Chuck Yeager and I each flew the X-3 three times.

It was one of the most difficult airplanes I have ever flown —and I am checked out in 122 different models and makes. It was considerably underpowered, which necessitated a very long take-off run, while in the air its high wing-loading—the ratio of weight to lift—gave it stall characteristics that were almost critical and approached the point where it would not support its own weight in flight. The combination of high wing-loading and inadequate power also made it difficult to land without stalling or losing control.

Bridgeman briefed me thoroughly on the airplane and in addition I spent several hours in the cockpit studying the instruments and controls. Distinct control problems resulted from its combination of very long fuselage and extra-short wings. Longitudinal control was sensitive and the airplane pitched up and down on the slightest provocation. I noticed during some of Bridgeman's early flights that he was prone to overcontrol because the airplane was so sensitive, and when he did the X-3 would always begin pitching.

The wings had both leading and trailing edge flaps to give it additional lift during take-off and landing. In fact, leading edge flaps were required after take-off until the airplane had attained an air speed close to 350 knots. I found this out on my first flight, when I retracted them at 300 knots and at the same time began a turn back toward the base. The X-3 immediately began to buffet and stall because the wings could not support the weight, and I had to level out and continue flying straight ahead.

I climbed to about 37,000 feet, where I made some maneuvers, put the airplane in a dive and went supersonic. However, to get any worthwhile speed it needed the afterburner. This burned up fuel fast and limited flight to less than an hour. After more maneuvers I returned to Edwards for my landing.

At 5,000 feet I extended leading edge flaps and chopped the engines back to a low power setting. Then I turned into my downwind leg and extended trailing edge flaps and landing gear. As I did so I began sinking like a rock. At once I applied full power and pulled my gear up, and not until I was turning into my final approach did I again extend the gear. I made two more flights in the X-3 without any real trouble, but at the same time realizing I had a very difficult airplane to fly. This was my first experience with an extremely high wing-loaded, underpowered airplane.

Among its responsibilities as a member nation of NATO, the North Atlantic Treaty Organization, the United States maintained armed forces in England and Europe and bought defense materiel abroad in our offshore procurement program. As part of this program the Air Force evaluated the best foreign aircraft for possible purchase overseas. To conduct this evaluation, several teams of test pilots were sent to Europe at intervals to fly new jet planes available in other

NATO countries. I was on the team that went to England to evaluate the Gloster Javelin and the Hawker Hunter.

Our first stop was the Gloster Aircraft Company at Gloucester, where William Waterton, their chief test pilot, introduced us to their airplane. It is a delta-wing air-defense fighter built for all-weather use. It is not a true delta, as it has 55-degree sweepback instead of 60-degree. A horizontal stabilizer with elevators was mounted high on the vertical tail. The elevator and ailerons were power-boosted but not enough, and in addition the elevator lost its effectiveness at high speeds.

It was a fairly easy airplane to fly. It had a short take-off and landing roll and a good rate of climb, and we felt it had a lot of potential. Although it was Mach-limited in level flight, with speed comparable to our F-89 and F-94 interceptors, by thinning out the wings and equipping the engines with afterburning, we thought its performance could be increased considerably. Aside from the limited effectiveness of the elevator at high speeds the Javelin was easy to maneuver, and we felt its faults could be overcome by redesigning the tail surfaces.

We found very little instrumentation in the planes we tested, and it appeared that the engineers got their flight data almost entirely from the pilot's comments. In fact, with the instruments available, we were not certain exactly how fast the Javelin could fly. To determine the actual speed we paced it with American Sabre Jets and in this way obtained an approximation of the true speed of the airplane, which was around 650 miles an hour.

In any event, we were unable to get it supersonic. At that time it was restricted to Mach .93 because of a flutter that had developed in high-speed dives, damaging the rudder. We were told that the airplane had gone through the sound barrier, but under the circumstances we could not substantiate this information. Despite these difficulties, however, we reported that the Javelin had a good potential for growth and if the manufacturer continued to develop it we thought it was worthy of consideration for procurement as an all-weather interceptor.

From Gloster we went to the Hawker-Siddeley Company at Dunsford to fly a new day fighter, the Hawker Hunter. Here we met Neville Duke, their famous test pilot, whom I immediately took a liking to, and made several flights in the airplane. It was a beautiful plane to fly and I felt at home in it immediately. It was highly maneuverable and speed was a little better than our F-86 Sabre Jet. But the 86 was an old airplane by now, and we were reluctant to recommend the procurement of a new day fighter like the Hunter which did not offer a substantial performance increase. However, it was a nice airplane to fly, and today is one of the main front-line fighters of the Royal Air Force.

The Hunter certainly is superior to the Russian-built MIG-15, the enemy's best fighter plane in the Korean War. Upon my return from England I tested the MIG that had been flown out of Korea and found it to be badly overrated. At Mach .96 it was all I could do to pull out of a dive and at anything above this speed it would become uncontrollable. The Russians and Chinese apparently realized this, because they had placarded the airplane not to dive above Mach .93. They had also instrumented it to extend its dive brakes automatically at Mach .93, this preventing the pilot from going any faster.

Mig 15

Chuck Yeager had already demonstrated that the MIG was not supersonic. When he evaluated the airplane on Okinawa soon after it was captured, he dove it straight down from 55,000 feet and could not get it up to Mach 1 in a dive. It was a good airplane for shooting down B-29 bombers, which it was designed for, but it was not the equal of the F-86. By American standards, it was a fairly crude airplane. It lacked automatic pressurization and the pilot had to adjust the cockpit pressure manually as he flew higher. He was usually cold; the airplane had a poor heating system and the canopy and windshield usually frosted over, giving him poor visibility. All in all, the MIG-15 was not a good airplane, regardless of what some pilots said about it.

Of course, the MIG-15 has been followed by newer models and aircraft with improved performance. The Russian Air Force today is equipped with modern jet fighters and bombers that are believed to be comparable to anything flying.

For example, published reports in this country indicate that at least three day fighters, two all-weather fighters, and several modern bombers are in production and in service in the Soviet Union. Day fighters include the MIG-17 jet, a swept-wing airplane with a top speed of 750 miles an hour; the MIG-19 twin-jet *Farmer*, capable of 900 miles an hour; and the MIG-21 *Super Farmer*, a single-jet airplane with a top speed of 1,200 miles an hour.

Soviet all-weather fighters in service include the Yak 25 *Flashlight* and the supersonic *Super Flashlight*, both swept-wing airplanes with two jet engines mounted on the wings. Several jet bombers are in service with the Red Air Force; these are designed for tactical, medium-range, and long-range requirements. The twin-engined *Blowlamp* is a sweptwing tactical bomber with a speed of over 700 miles an hour. The 600 mph *Badger* is slower but has more range and compares favorably with the American B-47, although it has only two engines against six in the B-47. For long range the Russians have the four-engine *Bison* jet bomber, comparable in performance to our B-52, which has twice as many engines.

We have nothing like the Russian *Bear*, a very large turboprop bomber weighing around 300,000 pounds with a top speed of 650 miles an hour. Despite its size, it is very fast, and can fly 8,000 miles without refueling.

*   *   *

We lost thirteen test pilots killed in flying accidents during the six years I spent at Edwards. Some of these accidents were caused by pilot error, some by maintenance error, and some by structural failure. These pilots, however, are not expendable, and on each occasion when a pilot was lost it was shocking, especially because they worked for me and were my friends.

On one test in an all-weather interceptor, the pilot suffered an engine failure at low altitude and attempted to glide the airplane back to the base for a deadstick landing. Normally in the event of an engine failure in a high-speed airplane at low altitude, it is best to bail out rather than run the risk of not getting back to the airfield; however, the pilot tried to save the airplane he was flying. But he lost altitude too rapidly to reach the lake bed and crashed in the desert.

On a high-speed test in another airplane, we were trying to dive the airplane at supersonic speeds to determine its handling characteristics at high Mach numbers. On this test the airplane failed to come out of the dive, but instead of bailing out and saving his life, the pilot stayed with the plane in an effort to pull it out of the dive. He was unable to do so and it crashed into the ground.

On another test in an advanced type of fighter-bomber, we badly needed information on performance for the pilot's handbook. The test pilot lost his engine over rough ground, but knowing the vital importance of the airplane for future testing, instead of bailing out he tried to save it by landing on a small dirt field in the vicinity. However, the speed of the plane made it impossible for him to get down on the short runway, and he overshot the field and crashed.

In the event that an airplane crashed at the base, we had arranged a system with the chief telephone operator at Edwards to prevent rumors and false reports from reaching the wives of our test pilots. We made up a list of these women and gave it to the telephone office. Whenever a plane crashed, one of my operations officers immediately called the chief telephone operator and instructed her to stop all incoming calls to persons he designated on this list.

In this way, we stopped any rumors or incorrect reports from reaching the wife of the pilot until we knew definitely who had crashed, the full extent of his injuries, if any, and whether he had survived the crash. In the event he was killed, we also made certain that his wife would get the news in a personal visit, when we could do more to help her stand the shock. Needless to say, it is a great blow to a woman in any event, but most test pilots' wives learned to live with danger.

As chief of flight test operations and because of my relationship as their superior officer, it was my duty to break the sad news to their wives and families. This was one of the hardest parts of my job at Edwards—to go to the homes of these men and tell their wives they would never return.

Naturally these women were broken up, but in most cases they were good troopers. They were aware of the dangers of our profession and perhaps had subconsciously prepared themselves for such a disaster. On several occasions when I had the unpleasant duty of telling a wife that her husband was dead, I was proud of the way these women were able to control their feelings and carry on in a highly commendable manner.

The pilots were also exceptional. They had a devotion to duty and a love of flying that has never been surpassed. They volunteered for the job, of course, and did not have to be test pilots except through their own desire. But they knew it was their job to make airplanes safer and more acceptable for operational use, whatever the risk to themselves—the best airplanes for their missions that we could possibly give the Air Force.

When they were assigned to the section, I always told them to expect and accept extra risks. If something went wrong with the airplane they were testing, I wanted them to do everything they could to bring it back so we could find the trouble and correct it. Naturally, if they were certain they could not bring it back, they were to bail out and save themselves—no airplane is worth the life of the pilot. But otherwise I expected them to take more risks than would normally be expected.

As for myself, I was fortunate in not having any serious accidents. In ten years as a test pilot at Wright Field and Edwards, I was never injured in an airplane, and I think this was the result of my length of time in the business. As I gained flying experience I grew to know the signs of trouble and was able to evaluate it when it occurred. In this way, I was able to take action to counteract it or return to base and land. I could have bailed out of some of the airplanes I brought back, but every one was important, and if there was any chance to save them I always tried.

One of the important things that came out of the Air Force flight test program at Edwards was the new prestige of the military test pilot. In the old days, the manufacturers were inclined to look down on Air Force test pilots as inferior in judgment, ability, and experience. But with the advent of the Flight Test Center, where we flew many different types and makes of aircraft, our experience increased and we became better known. We were in a position to fly every kind of plane and over the years we became the best judges of the faults and advantages of all.

We knew then that Air Force test pilots were more experienced and could sit in better judgment than any civilian pilot, however competent and qualified. We had more varied experience and thus were in a better position to judge what was good and bad about an airplane. Contractor pilots, who on the whole were restricted to flying airplanes built by their employers, did not have the same opportunity to keep abreast of the whole field of aeronautical design and development. As a result of our work at Edwards, the military test pilot today is conceded to be the best in his profession.

9

Mach 2.3

After the Bell X-1 rocket plane broke the sound barrier in October, 1947, the Air Force gave Bell Aircraft Corporation another contract to build improved models of this history-making airplane. Five more planes were ordered—the X-1 No. 3, also known as Queenie, which was similar to the No. 1 and No. 2 airplanes except for a different fuel system; and the X-1A, B, C, and D. Each was intended for flight tests in a specific research program. The C airplane, which was designed to test aircraft armament in supersonic flight, was canceled later when the F-86 Sabrejet turned out to be capable of supersonic speeds and provided the same information.

Of the six X-1's that were built, only three are still in existence. The original X-1 completed more than 100 flights and was turned over to the Smithsonian Institution in Washington, D.C. The X-1 No. 2, which was built at the same time for the National Advisory Committee for Aeronautics, was redesignated the X-1E and is still flying. NACA also got the X-1B after completion of the Air Force high-speed research program and is still flying it. The other airplanes have been destroyed. The X-1 No. 3 caught fire on the ground prior to its first flight and burned, injuring Joe Cannon, a Bell pilot who later became Bell's chief test pilot. The X-1D and X-1A both caught fire in mid-air explosions and were jettisoned from the mother ship without loss of life.

The A, B, and D airplanes were identical and all three had much higher performance than the original X-1. Like the X-1 No. 3, they had a fuel pump and low-pressure tanks. In this system, a gas-driven turbine pump was used to force fuel into the combustion chambers. In addition, the fuselage had been stretched out nearly five feet. This gave them more fuel capacity, which increased their flight endurance to 4.2 minutes under full power. Fully fueled for launching, each weighed over 16,000 pounds. Because they could stay in the air longer, they were capable of flying to new speeds and heights.

In 1951, about the time I became chief of flight test operations, the new X-1's began arriving at Edwards to begin the various research programs for which they were designed. As so-called "chief test pilot" for the Air Force, I was responsible for the details of military participation in these flights. I worked with the Bell company and NACA in setting up and conducting the various flight tests. In addition, I flew some of the tests myself and also assigned other Air Force pilots to fly them.

With these airplanes, my pilots and I were among the first men to fly twice as fast as sound. A few years earlier, before Chuck Yeager proved it could be done, the speed of sound itself had been beyond our reach. Since then Bill Bridgeman and Scott Crossfield in the Douglas Skyrocket had surpassed his mark. Now using the results of their experience and our own knowledge and confidence, we set new speed records and flew to heights never before reached by man.

Our achievements were made despite initial setbacks that delayed us many months. Fires of unknown origin destroyed the first two airplanes to reach Edwards and held up work on the remaining two craft. Both the X-1D and the X-1 No. 3 were lost before we could test their capabilities. As a result, it was December of 1953 before Chuck Yeager was able to fly the X-1A to a new record of Mach 2.42, nearly two-and-a-half times the speed of sound. And it was May of 1954 before Major Kit Murray flew the same airplane to an altitude record of 94,000 feet.

The X-1D, the first in the series to be completed, was brought to Edwards in 1951 to continue high-speed flight research being conducted with the X-1 rocket planes. Like the X-1 No. 3 that preceded it and the A and B models that followed, it had the new low-pressure fuel system, greater fuel capacity, a redesigned cockpit for better visibility, and a new jettisonable canopy that permitted the pilot to enter and leave the cockpit through the top of the airplane.

We in the Air Force had been following with considerable interest the progress of a civilian test program on the Navy's new rocket plane, the Douglas Skyrocket, which the manufacturer was conducting at the Air Force test center at Edwards. This was a sweptwing airplane capable of supersonic performance. The No. 2 airplane, the D-558-2, had a rocket engine similar to the X-1 power plant and used the same fuel combination of liquid oxygen and water alcohol.

Under the Air Force policy of cooperating with private contractors on their test programs, I flew chase plane for the Douglas pilots many times, first with Gene Mays and later with Bill Bridgeman when he took over the Skyrocket testing. As a result of this close association, we were aware of the fact that they were getting up near the X-1 speed record, and we knew they would beat it if they could.

Had the Skyrocket been purely a Douglas project, perhaps we would not have felt so competitive about it, but as it was sponsored and built for the Navy, naturally some feeling of interservice rivalry was bound to exist. In these circumstances, we wanted to keep pace with the Skyrocket and if possible stay ahead.

At this time the speed record was 967 miles an hour, set by Chuck Yeager in the original X-1 in 1948. Nearly three years had gone by and it was only a matter of time before the Skyrocket beat this record. But the X-1D was ready now, built to fly nearly twice that fast, and with the higher performance of the new airplane, we had a chance to set another record that would be much harder to beat. Under the circumstances, we lost no time in trying.

Bell flew half a dozen tests to prove the new rocket ship's flying characteristics and tested the rocket engine in runups on the ground. Then I was selected to take it up and see what it could do wide open.

This was my first flight in the X-1D and the first step in a new program we hoped would lead us past Mach 2. As such, it held more than ordinary significance for the Air Force. General Albert Boyd, commander of the Air Force Flight Test Center, had chosen to fly chase today, accompanied by the director of flight test, Lt. Col. Gust Askounis, in another F-86. Captain Sellers flew the B-50 and Major Jack Ridley, the flight engineer on the original X-1 project, came along as copilot in the bomber to lend his long experience in any problems that might develop. Wendell Moore, the boyish-looking Bell rocket expert who was the X-1 rocket engineer, also accompanied us personally to supervise final preparations for drop.

After take-off I sat around chatting with Ridley and Moore while the B-50 mother ship climbed in the familiar slow spiral, straining for altitude with eight tons of X-1 in its belly. I wore the cumbersome pressure suit needed on rocket flights and carried a pressure helmet in my hand. At 10,000 feet Ridley helped me put on my helmet and adjust it. Then I climbed down through the bomb bay and entered the rocket ship to begin my cockpit check.

I noticed immediately that the X-1 was losing the nitrogen source pressure required to actuate the various pressure systems. Pressure on the gauge was down to 1,500 pounds and falling. Disgusted and disappointed, I climbed back up in the B-50 to discuss the problem with Ridley and Moore. When the leak continued despite our efforts to stop it, we reluctantly admitted we would have to abort the flight.

I took off my pressure helmet and loosened the top half of my pressure suit in order to move more freely and went back down in the X-1 again to jettison the water alcohol and liquid oxygen. Moore was on the edge of the bomb bay and looking into the cockpit. Standing on the seat in the X-1, I steadied myself with my left hand on the edge of the cockpit, while with my right hand I reached down and turned the valve that pressurized the liquid oxygen tank.

As I did so a deafening blast shook the X-1 and nearly knocked me down. Startled and momentarily numbed by the shock, I straightened up in the cockpit and looked around. To my dismay I saw a stream of fire from the top of the rocket ship pouring into the bomb bay of the B-50.

Nobody said anything. Ridley instinctively went for the emergency drop handle in the bomb bay to jettison the X-1 before its fuel exploded. At the same instant I vaulted clear of the plane in one leap into the bomber. I went sailing right over the top of Moore, who was still crouched in the opening, and squarely against Ridley, who had seized the emergency handle to drop the X-1.

The force of my mad exit knocked him forward into the

cockpit of the B-50—luckily for us all, because the locking pins in the bomb shackles had not been removed. Had he pulled the emergency drop handle, the burning plane would have fallen on the locking pins and jammed.

As the first blast blew off the landing gear doors, the landing gear dropped from the wheel wells and the doors fell toward the ground. Seeing the doors tumbling through the sky, General Boyd and Colonel Askounis realized at once that we had had an explosion, and General Boyd came on the air immediately telling us to drop the X-1.

Without my helmet I lacked radio communication and could not hear him, but we were well aware of the need for haste. Ridley and I jumped to our feet and I yelled at him to jettison the airplane. Reaching forward in the B-50 cockpit he grasped the normal drop lever and pulled it hard with both hands. As he did so the bomb shackles snapped open and the burning X-1 with its load of explosive propellants fell free and plummeted earthward.

As a result of this disaster and the subsequent fire that destroyed the X-1 No. 3, the new X-1 test program was set back nearly two years. Without an airplane to fly, further performance tests had to be suspended while the remaining airplanes were redesigned.

Bell engineers spent many months at the factory in an effort to determine the cause of these explosions. On the chance that the propellant system was to blame, it was once more completely changed, with cylinder tanks replacing the nitrogen tube bundles in the earlier planes. This did not solve the problem, as later events were to prove. In the meantime, the last two X-1 airplanes went back on the shelf until they were considered safe.

It was nearly two years later, in the summer of 1953, that the X-1 program was resumed. The X-1A, one of the two remaining planes, was completed and shipped to Edwards. At the same time Chuck Yeager returned from Command and Staff School, where he had been a student, and I selected him to fly it.

I felt that Chuck was best qualified to fly the new airplane because he was the most experienced rocket pilot in the Air Force. I had recently made him assistant chief of flight test operations because of his outstanding knowledge and experience. As his superior officer, I might have chosen the X-1A assignment myself, but I was more interested in another project. The Bell X-2, a newer and faster rocket ship, was nearing completion and held greater attraction for me at this time. Although the first X-2 which I flew in 1952 had been destroyed a few months earlier, the second airplane would be ready in a few months and I wanted to wait for that.

With Yeager as pilot, we once more began the X-1 high-speed program that had ended in near-tragedy when the No. 3 airplane burned to ashes on the desert floor. Our goal was still to fly this airplane to Mach 2 or beyond, and Chuck was the man to do it. By this time the old X-1 record had long since been broken by both Bridgeman and Crossfield, so there was no question of keeping ahead of them. Our problem now was trying to catch up.

Chuck began flying the X-1A in September, 1953, slowly working up to the higher Mach numbers. As he approached Mach 2, or twice the speed of sound, we found that the stability of the airplane began to deteriorate. The X-1A would start rolling back and forth from side to side at high supersonic speeds, and at the same time it developed a yawing motion resulting from lack of directional stability.

This did not concern us unduly, as wind tunnel studies had indicated that stability of the X-1A would slowly deteriorate at high Mach numbers. Stability of this model had been designed to be positive up to Mach 1.9, while its improved design and more powerful engine gave it the potential of exceeding this speed by a considerable margin. For this reason, we expected to have control problems. Chuck pushed the speed up in small increments beyond Mach 2, and by observing great care he was able to maintain control with a reasonable degree of safety.

By December he had flown the X-1A up to Mach 2 several times. We had matched Bridgeman and Crossfield even money, and now we raised the bid. Confident that we had a winner, Chuck took it up again on December 12 to see what it could do wide open.

Jack Ridley and Kit Murray flew chase planes and Major Harold Russell flew the B-29. Russell dropped him at 32,000 feet and Chuck got a good rocket light. He climbed to 45,000 feet on three rocket chambers, his speed between Mach .8 and .9, and at 45,000 feet began to round out. After going

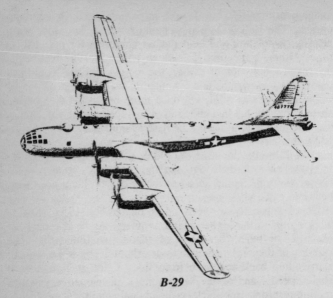

B-29

supersonic, he pulled the nose up again and lit his fourth rocket chamber. At 65,000 feet his speed was Mach 1.25 and he began to level out and accelerate. At 75,000 feet he was straight and level and speed was Mach 2.42. This was a true air speed of 1,650 miles an hour, faster than any human being had ever flown.

We know now that Chuck ran out of control. Flying at Mach 2.42 in an airplane designed to have positive stability only up to Mach 1.9, he was in a situation without any precedent. In such a situation, the best test pilot in the world—which he is—would have no previous experience to guide him. He was dealing with unknown conditions and there was nothing to go by when he met them. Feeling his way into space, at 1,650 miles an hour he lost control and the X-1 uncorked—went out of control.

The airplane began tumbling through the stratosphere at terrible speeds, rolling and tossing, and Chuck was thrown violently about in the cockpit at forces up to fourteen times the pull of gravity. He and the X-1 were subjected to stresses never before encountered in flight. Somehow both lived through it. As the airplane tumbled it fell to lower altitudes, and 30,000 feet later in denser air its momentum slackened. As it did so the wild gyrations lessened and Chuck was able to regain command.

Badly beaten up, but still conscious, he began flying the airplane once more. By now his speed had dropped below Mach 1 and the X-1A was controllable. With Ridley and Murray guiding him down, he returned to base and made a successful landing on the dry lake bed. It was the first time that I ever saw Chuck badly shaken.

From this flight we decided we had better not experiment further at extreme Mach numbers and canceled further speed runs until we knew more about control problems at high speeds. While we waited for the engineers to tell us why Chuck got into trouble, we began an alternate program to set a new altitude record in the X-1.

The pilot selected was Major Kit Murray, a former test pilot in my division. He had been moved to a new assignment in the operations section without getting any of the so-called "gravy" flights. Kit was eager for an opportunity to make a contribution, so he was chosen to conduct the high-altitude tests. Bill Bridgeman's record of 79,000 feet in the Douglas Skyrocket was the mark he had to beat.

Kit was thoroughly familiar with the X-1 program, having flown chase plane many times for Chuck and myself, and was well qualified for the new assignment. Realizing, however, that he could get into trouble as Yeager did, we approached his flights with extreme caution.

We knew, of course, that if Kit got the X-1 into a high angle of attack and suffered a loss of power he could expect possible loss of control; and if this happened at higher altitudes where the air was thinner, he would have even more difficulty regaining control of the airplane. To prevent a recurrence of Yeager's mishap, if possible, we changed the flight plan accordingly.

The first part of Kit's flight was identical, up to Mach 1.25 at 65,000 feet. Upon reaching this speed and altitude, however, instead of leveling out and accelerating, he continued his climb. He watched his Machmeter carefully, let his speed increase gradually as he gained altitude, and was still under Mach 2 when he experienced rocket burnout at extreme altitude.

Instead of trying to zoom even higher, he started the nose of the airplane down and continued through in the normal ballistic curve. Had he kept the nose up, he could have gone higher; it is possible the X-1 would have reached 100,000 feet. But again we were confronted with the possibility of loss of control if he stalled out in a steep climb and fell backward toward the ground. We wanted to play this one safe and use proper techniques and not take chances.

Despite our precautions, the airplane went out of control. In thin air of the upper atmosphere, the plummeting rocket ship uncorked and fell 40,000 feet before Kit was able to get control again. Because he was going considerably slower than Yeager when he tumbled, fortunately he did not take as bad a beating. After regaining control he returned safely to base and landed, having flown higher than any other human being.

We learned from these two flights that the stability of the X-1A decayed at high speeds, but it could be controlled to a certain degree. If the airplane started to roll to the right and we applied left aileron, it would respond very slowly, and then the inertia of the rolling motion or moment would carry it past the level wing position and continue in the opposite direction. You would then apply right aileron after the wing had continued past the neutral point and started rolling to the left and it had no effect whatsoever.

The same way with yaw control. The airplane started to yaw to the right, you would apply left rudder, and it would respond very slowly to left rudder. Then when the airplane was straight again and you released the left rudder, it would continue yawing past the neutral point to the left. At that time you would put in right rudder but it would only aggravate this moment.

In other words, you would try to stop the yawing moment, and end up overshooting. Then back and forth, back and forth, with the yawing moment becoming greater and at the same time the lateral overcontrol becoming more pronounced. On many of their early flights, both Murray and Yeager found themselves making complete 360-degree rolls, accompanied by extremely high yaw angles, before they could regain control of the airplane.

Out of their experience we learned to fly the airplane better by using new control techniques. If a roll started we applied opposite aileron, and when the airplane began to respond, we either released the control pressure or even applied opposite control. In this manner, after a certain amount of experience, we learned to control the airplane adequately. At this point we felt we could go back to higher altitudes and higher Mach numbers in safety.

Although the X-1A was turned over to NACA for other purposes, we had an opportunity to try our knowledge in the X-1B, which came to Edwards in the fall of 1954. It lacked instrumentation, but we used it to check out more pilots and give them rocket experience, planning to turn it over to NACA also after our familiarization program had been completed. I used the opportunity to gain additional rocket experience myself, in preparation for my coming flights in the Bell X-2. After a checkout and familiarization flight on October 8, I took it up again to see how fast it would fly.

When I told Colonel Hanes I planned to go balls-out, it was his startled opinion that a maximum speed run would be unduly hazardous. This was the first time we had tried to push the X-1 beyond Mach 2 since Chuck Yeager's record flight a year before. Colonel Hanes had not forgotten what happened to Chuck on that flight when the airplane went out of control at high speeds, and naturally he was concerned about the same thing happening again. As a result, he thought I was taking an unnecessary risk and said he felt I should restrict my speed to Mach 1.5.

I told him I thought this was being overly cautious. I pointed out that the F-100 would fly to Mach numbers of 1.5 and if I wanted to reach those speeds I didn't have to do it in a rocket ship. I said I wanted to fly the X-1B to get some experience in higher Mach numbers where I would be flying the X-2 on forthcoming tests. I also observed that we had learned a lot about the high-speed control problems of the X-1 since Chuck's flight and this time I believed the airplane would be controllable. I assured him that I loved to live as much as the next man and had no desire to take unnecessary risks. If I felt I was approaching an uncontrolled condition I would immediately cut the rocket engines and not go any faster. After some argument, mostly on my part, he told me all right, I could go as fast as I wanted.

Chuck Yeager had left Edwards for an overseas assignment

so I no longer had the benefit of his advice and guidance. However, I well remembered all he had told me of his wild ride in the X-1A twelve months earlier. If experience was any teacher, I had no intention of letting the same thing happen to me.

The flight was called for seven o'clock in the morning of December 2. I left home before six and drove to the flight line, where the ground crew was fueling the rocket plane. As it was wintertime, the sun had not yet risen. Skies were overcast and rain fell intermittently. Because of weather conditions the flight was delayed and I got in the Bell jeep to wait for a better report.

With Jack Ridley, the X-1 engineer, and Wendell Moore, the Bell rocket engineer, I went over the flight plan again. Go fast, but take it slow. Above all, don't experiment. Don't get into new situations where the problems are unknown. Then Harold Russell, the B-29 pilot, signaled that he was ready, and we got out of the car and boarded the waiting plane.

It was almost ten o'clock when Russell released his brakes and the big bomber thundered down the runway with the little rocket ship fastened in its belly and lifted heavily off the ground. As wheels and flaps came up I left my take-off position in the bombardier's seat and went back to the bomb bay where Moore and Ridley were supervising "lox" (liquid oxygen) topoff procedures. As the B-29 drove its slow spiral upward I sat down by the X-1 control panel and we talked intermittently during breaks in the routine.

At 10,000 feet now, I entered the X-1 and began my cockpit check. The cockpit was unheated and the temperature was well below freezing by this time. Soon all metal surfaces on the controls and instrument panel were covered over with a thin coating of frost. Despite heavy gloves and flying boots, my fingers and toes began to lose all feeling.

When we had finished the check list and all instruments and controls checked satisfactorily, Major Ridley came down from the B-29 and helped me place the heavy canopy in position. I locked it securely and he climbed back in the bomber. Overcast was improving as predicted by weather, and soon we received final radio clearance to proceed with the drop. Shortly before 11 A.M. Major Russell dropped me at 30,000 feet in a westerly direction and the X-1B fell free in brilliant sunlight.

Now all discomforts of being cold and cramped up in the freezing cockpit were forgotten as my insensate fingers flipped three rocket switches on the control panel and three rocket chambers roared into life. Like a stone flung from a giant slingshot the falling airplane hurtled forward, shock waves blasting from its engine exhaust and a plume of white fire streaming behind against the blue desert sky. "Three chambers —good!" Kit Murray's familiar voice came through my earphones from his F-100 chase plane to the right and below me. Even as he spoke the X-1 shot away from him like a bullet and I pulled its pointed nose up sharply in a screaming climb.

Briefly my eyes swept the dials staring at me from the frosted instrument panel. Machmeter reading point 8, altimeter reading 40,000. The airspeed indicator continued to wind slowly as I held the airplane in its steep ascent. My arms labored against the control stick as the X-1 protested this unnatural limitation on its wild energy. Unfeelingly I forced the control surfaces into the predetermined pattern. *In a minute*, I said silently, admiring the untamed spirit of this primordial animal straining against the leash. It trembled under my hands as the stick forces mounted. *In a minute you can fly*, I said. *Wait a minute*.

The X-1 buffeted sharply as speed reached Mach .9. This was all routine. Altimeter read 45,000 and Machmeter near 1. Then I pushed the control stick forward and the nose of the airplane dropped toward the far horizon. As it leveled out the rocket ship accelerated and shot through the sound barrier like a bullet through glass. The needle in the airspeed indicator was winding faster now. Buffet slackened off and noise abruptly ceased. As the air pressures eased on the control surfaces the stick relaxed in my hands and stopped trembling.

Altimeter was 55,000 and Mach 1.25. Carefully I pulled the nose up again and pointed it toward the sky. Then I flipped the fourth rocket switch and the fourth rocket chamber lighted with perceptible forward thrust. Supersonic now, the X-1 protested briefly, then settled back in its smooth stride. Flying faster than sound, angle of flight made little difference to the fleeting ship. Climbing now, its speed continued to increase.

Altimeter again and altitude 65,000. Now the Machmeter held my steadfast gaze. As I pushed the stick forward the

Mach needle jumped upward and the stick forces mounted. The whole airplane seemed to protest my puny interference as I strove to divert it from its upward rush. Still it struggled to climb higher as I forced it grimly downward toward level flight.

Now the X-1 began the dread roll from wing to wing, and the slow fishlike yaw of the tail from side to side. I moved the control surfaces delicately, flying by feel now, sensitive to touch. This was a leaf in a tempest, a cork in a flooding stream. Lightly I led it, carefully I caught it. Over the wing went, over and back. Then the other wing, over and back. The tail followed fishlike behind me, weaving softly in my wake.

Except where the white light of heaven struck its exposed surfaces, the cockpit lay in unearthly shadow at 70,000 feet. Glowing in noonday darkness, I saw on the panel the instruments that guided me. Flight was level now. A sea shell in space, the X-1 swept forward irresistibly on the infinite tide. Four rocket chambers all burning, speed was Mach 2, and still the airplane continued to accelerate.

Time was now. Here was forever. Suspended in time, I felt infinity opening before me. Could I refuse it? Should I turn back? Drugged in a dream, for a moment I did nothing. What unknowns waited to marvel me? Mortal though I was, for one awful instant I desired to go on.

Wrenching my will painfully back from the abyss that beckoned, I saw then the precipice on which I tottered and turned consciously toward the world I knew. I wanted that world, I knew now, and to it I must return. Reality once more commanded my movements as I began the familiar pattern which would bring me back to life on earth.

Power could save me—power that stabilizes an aircraft in flight. Had sudden loss of power hurled Yeager into the void? Could I come back safely if power helped me? Speed was now Mach 2.1. Following a predetermined plan, my obedient fingers deliberately released the rocket switches on the control panel, slowly yet decisively, one by one. As the rocket chambers cut out and stopped firing, acceleration decreased evenly, a barely perceptible loss of thrust that could not upset the delicate equilibrium of my headlong flight.

In the cockpit I still led the airplane gently, easily. With three chambers off, the last rocket burned out of fuel at Mach 2.3 and shut down. I was aware then that I was flying very fast, in the absolute silence and absence of motion in a world alone. My speed was 1,519 miles an hour. My mind toyed with the thought that for me this was the fastest yet—only Yeager had flown faster. Then I dismissed it from my mind.

There was no more time for dreaming as I concentrated on flying the airplane. In the rolling moment the wings were still rolling 70 degrees about their axis and the tail was yawing 10 degrees from line of flight. Very carefully now I went to work on the controls as speed continued to slacken, trying to get the wings level again and steady the tail. Being preoccupied this way, there was no time now to look around or speculate on the importance of my achievement.

Earth-bound once more, I broke radio silence at last to report my speed and altitude in code. It was a toy world I talked to, where disembodied voices whispered at me through space. I told them of the rolling and turning behavior of the airplane and how I was trying to control it. Then I stopped, realizing I could not explain. How could they understand what I was trying to tell them? On the jigsaw-puzzle landscape where I would make my sure landfall, familiar names spoke words from another planet.

As I began the wide turn from Mach 2 and the long descent from 13 miles above the earth that would lead me back home, I felt very good about this flight. Not only had it made me the second fastest man alive, but more important, it bore out my theory that this airplane was controllable at high Mach numbers. In my pilot's report I commented later that I thought this airplane could be flown safely up to Mach 2.5. With more pilot experience and by using a cautious approach, I recommended that NACA could fly both the X-1A and the X-1B to the speed limits of the airplane.

Even more important, we had learned things that would help us fly still faster airplanes in the future. The little X-1 left permanent milestones in the sky. Information that we gained on flight techniques at high speed would aid others who followed us along that high way. And coming in over the dry lake bed for my last X-1 landing, I felt personally benefited and grateful. Because of a handful of rocket pioneers, flying unknown airplanes from this desert valley, the world had new dimensions. And what I had learned would help me meet the greater challenge of the Bell X-2, which soon would fly under its own power for the first time.

X-2

The X-2 rocket ship began in October, 1945, as a proposal to the Army Air Forces by Bell Aircraft Corporation to conduct research on the performance of a sweptwing aircraft in high-speed flight. Unlike the straight-wing X-1, which had been started a year earlier, the new plane would have wings swept back at a 40-degree angle from the fuselage to the wing-tips. Secrets of German research in sweepback had been captured in Europe five months earlier and brought back to this country for possible use on new jet aircraft scheduled for postwar production. The German studies indicated that a sweptwing airplane could fly faster because it had less drag, which we already knew from our own experience would be a serious problem in high-speed jets. The sweepback theory soon proved itself in the North American F-86 fighter plane and the Boeing B-47 bomber, which were so good they are still the backbone of our combat Air Force twelve years later. It was Bell's proposal to test sweepback at even higher speeds in a rocket ship. From this idea came the X-2, which broke all records for speed and altitude in a piloted aircraft.

The Air Force was deeply impressed by the scope and daring of the X-2 proposal, and equally confident that Bell had the ability and determination to see it through. Four months later the Pentagon issued a letter contract to begin design studies and build two aircraft. The contract called for a rocket engine that Bell would also design and build. The airplane would fly to heights never before reached by powered aircraft.

This was in February, 1946, the same month I reported to Wright Field on my first assignment as a test pilot. As the X-2 and I were later to become so closely identified, it is interesting to me to look back and note that our careers had their beginning at the same time, so to speak. The new rocket ship was developed primarily by four Bell engineers—Bob Stanley, then chief engineer; Stan Smith, chief project engineer; Paul Emmons, chief aerodynamicist; and Bob Lapp, who later became project engineer. Stan Smith was the project engineer throughout the design phase, with Lapp as his assistant handling liaison in the experimental shop. As these two men lived with the airplane from the beginning, they deserve most credit for the success it later achieved.

The problems confronting Bell were fantastic. No rocket engine had ever been flown in an airplane—and no airplane had ever flown faster than sound. In 1946 the speed record was a mere 623 miles an hour, established by Colonel Albert Boyd. The swept wing was still a theory. Nothing was known about high-speed heating, which the X-2 was expected to encounter. No one knew if an airplane could be controlled at supersonic speeds—or how the control surfaces should be designed. In fact, nobody knew how to build the airplane itself.

Despite these handicaps, Bell engineers began design studies, using scale models of many different configurations in wind tunnels to test their behavior in various speed regimes. They had to build a wing thin enough to be supersonic, yet strong enough to carry the load. They had to build a tail surface smaller yet stronger, and also adjustable to compensate for trim changes in supersonic flight. They had to supply a booster system for controls, although they had no power source to operate it. Because rocket fuels burn very fast, they had to find room for 1,600 gallons of fuel in a 40-foot airplane—and under pressure because rockets use high-energy propellants.

They had to pressurize the cockpit to withstand altitudes never before reached—above 100,000 feet, where the sky is empty of air and temperature is absolute zero. If anything went wrong at these altitudes, they had to give the pilot a chance to escape with his life. They had to design an engine powerful enough to drive a Navy cruiser yet light enough to be carried in a 12,000-pound airplane. And after they did all these things, they had no idea how well the airplane would fly.

Because of changes in postwar procurement policies, the Air Force called in another contractor before the end of 1946, giving Curtiss-Wright Corporation at Wood-Ridge, New Jersey, the job of designing and building the rocket engine. It is just as well, because Bell had enough on its hands with the airframe alone.

Early in 1947, scale model tests in the wind tunnel laboratory of the National Advisory Committee for Aeronautics at Langley Field, Virginia, showed the X-2 ailerons were ineffective at high speeds, providing inadequate lateral control, and Bell had to modify the wing design. Beginning in 1947 and lasting two years, there was a long period of trouble developing methods of putting new metals together in an aircraft. Assuming everything else worked, the heat barrier still remained a problem, and it was to solve it that Bell sought metals that could stand high-speed heating. Ordinary aircraft aluminum got soft above 700 degrees Fahrenheit, where the X-2 was expected to fly—while harder metals like stainless steel had never been used in a modern high-speed airplane. It was 1949 before new metal-working methods had been developed sufficiently to go ahead with construction.

What Bell finally came up with was a 40-foot pressure vessel with the world's first throttleable rocket engine, permitting the pilot to increase or decrease his speed without shutting power off. It had wings of stainless steel and a fuselage of K-monel metal, an alloy of copper and nickel. These metals could withstand temperatures of 750 degrees Fahrenheit, which the X-2 was expected to meet. For fuel it burned water-alcohol and liquid oxygen, which boils at a temperature 300 degrees below zero—creating a temperature differential at maximum speed of 1,000 degrees between the inner and outer surfaces of the aircraft.

The X-2 had a completely power-boosted control system operated by a 300-pound lead-acid battery that burned itself out in thirty minutes. It had a 325-horsepower pump to drive the propellants from the fuel tanks to the engine at 600 gallons a minute. Fully tempered plate glass on the cockpit canopy was strong enough to stand 1,000-degree temperatures and tinted to shield the pilot from dangerous infrared rays in the upper atmosphere. The cockpit itself was carefully insulated to protect the pilot against heat transfer—it was not heated for obvious reasons. Should he be forced to leave the airplane at high altitudes, the pilot could blow the whole cockpit nose section off with an explosive charge twenty times the pull of gravity. If he survived this ejection from the airplane, the cockpit would protect him in pressurized air until it fell to lower altitudes, where he could leave the capsule itself.

Unlike the X-1, which had a conventional landing gear system, the X-2 was not intended to take off under its own power on the ground. To put tricycle wheels on the new plane would have added 1,000 pounds to its weight, reducing its performance so materially that it would not have been worth flying. Instead of conventional gear the X-2 had a 12-inch skid similar to an abbreviated ski, centered under the fuselage, with a small wheel in the nose to support its forward weight. With this gear the X-2 sat high about two feet off the ground.

Because it could not take off under its own power, the X-2 had to be dropped from a mother ship in flight. It was bigger and heavier than the first X-1, which weighed less than 14,000 pounds fully loaded, and to carry it aloft Bell used a B-50, which was a bigger version of the Boeing B-29. The B-50 is a four-engined bomber designed to carry a payload of 20,000 pounds to an altitude of 40,000 feet. However, the X-2 fully loaded weighed over 25,000 pounds, so we were never able to get much above 30,000 feet to drop it.

The B-50 was modified to carry the X-2 by cutting away the bomb bay so the rocket ship would fit up snugly inside. It was attached to the B-50 by two bomb shackles which the bomber pilot could release by tripping a lever in the cockpit. Sway braces running from the B-50 to the X-2 wings kept the rocket ship from rocking back and forth. There were also two sets of sway braces extending from the interior of the B-50 against both sides of the X-2 to hold it securely in position. Other modifications included an X-2 control panel in the B-50 and fuel tanks to carry an extra supply of liquid oxygen to refill the X-2 prior to drop.

* * *

In December, 1949, I was ordered to the Bell plant at Buffalo for an engineering conference on the X-1 project. This airplane was still uppermost in my thoughts. I had recently established an unofficial altitude record of 73,000 feet in the first airplane, before the test program was temporarily discontinued, and newer models under construction promised even better performance. We believed that they could fly even faster and higher than the original X-1, and I hoped to be one of the lucky pilots chosen to do it.

Hurrying through the Bell hangar the next morning, I was stopped in my tracks by the sight of an unfamiliar airplane I glimpsed by chance through a half-open door. It was bigger than the X-1, and its wings were swept back at a rakish angle of 40 degrees from its sleek body of shining metal. Without wheels, it sat on the floor on an odd-looking ski-shaped metal skid, supported by a large hydraulic strut. Bell employees stood around the unknown aircraft, watching as a static test rig was fitted carefully around its streamlined fuselage. I realized at once that this was the secret new Bell X-2.

Ignoring the "Keep Out" sign printed in large red letters above the doorway, I stepped into the room for a better look at the revolutionary new plane. Even without its rocket engine, which would not be ready for three more years, every line of this restless beauty cried speed. I could easily see it was a big step forward beyond the little X-1, which heretofore had been the ultimate in my ambitions. Give it the power it was designed for and it would run away from anything in the skies! Silently I promised myself to plan my future, if possible, to someday fly the X-2.

Static tests were completed in 1951 and in 1952 the X-2 was ready for glide tests carrying ballast. Still without an engine, but able to make a deadstick landing after an air drop, it was flown to Edwards Air Force Base in the B-50 mother ship in June, 1952, to test its stability and control in flight.

The pilot selected for the first flight was Skip Ziegler, Bell's chief test pilot. Skip was a tall, quiet Texan, a good engineer and a superb aviator. Like Jack Woolams and Tex Johnston, his predecessors, he had done his share of barnstorming and air racing. Also like Woolams and Johnston, he had flown and tested the X-1. After Tex left he took over the flight test program at Bell, and next to Yeager and myself was probably as well qualified as any pilot in the country in rocket ships.

Bell and the Air Force wanted to test the X-2 at Edwards because it was an experimental airplane that had never flown. By now six years of work and money totaling millions of dollars had been invested in this project. The fifteen miles of natural landing field on Rogers Dry Lake was none too good to protect such an investment when the X-2 first tried its wings.

On Skip's first flight, drop and letdown were satisfactory, but he ran into trouble on landing. As the X-2 touched down and began its slide along the ground, it veered sharply to the right and the nose slammed down abruptly on the desert floor. The little nose wheel, strained by the sudden impact, failed to caster and collapsed, and the skidding airplane dug its left wing-tip into the dirt, turned completely around, and came to a lurching stop. The X-2 went into the shop for repairs and Bell went into an immediate conference over the unexpected rough landing.

The upshot was a decision to improve directional control by modifying the airplane. As it had no wheels and therefore no brakes to slow it down, the best that Bell could do was keep it in a straight line until its momentum was expended. The solution they came up with was a pair of small auxiliary skids—we called them whisker skids—about midspan under each wing. It was felt these skids would maintain directional stability by giving the X-2 three points of support at the center of gravity of the airplane; and in the event it still turned sideways during its landing skid, they would at least keep the wings from dragging.

The whisker skids were installed in time for Skip's second flight and apparently accomplished their purpose. At any rate, he landed successfully. Feeling that the landing gear problem had been overcome, Bell invited the Air Force to make the third glide flight, and because of my interest in this airplane I was selected to be the pilot.

With a Bell civilian pilot at the controls, the B-50 took off at 7 A.M. and climbed to an altitude of 30,000 feet, where he dropped me. This was not a new experience for me, as I had made air drops many times previously in the X-1, but it never ceases to be a novel sensation. We had selected the wrong stabilizer setting today, however, giving the X-2 an excessive nose-down attitude after leaving the mother ship, and as a result the drop was more abrupt than usual.

I pulled up and made an approach to stall, felt the airplane buffet slightly in a stall warning, then dropped the nose and picked up speed once more. Next I did some pullups and aileron rolls to test out the control system. Because of the manual controls in use on the airplane at that time, the stick forces were quite heavy and the controls were hard to move.

Altitude was now 10,000 feet and I began to prepare for the familiar deadstick landing. I extended the main landing skid and nose wheel, then put down the whisker skids on the wings. However, the left skid failed to extend as I approached for my landing.

Knowing that the right skid would force the left wing down on the ground, I felt some alarm over the possibility of ground-looping when I touched down. At the high speed with which the X-2 landed, over 150 miles an hour, I did not relish the prospect of entering a flat spin on the ground in this airplane. I came in fast and flared out, flaps up to avoid undue wing turbulence that would decrease lateral control. As I set the airplane down, the contact with the ground jarred the left skid into extended position where it locked in place.

The airplane settled forward easily on the nose wheel and wing skids and slid smoothly across the desert floor. I maintained both lateral and directional control at all times and came to a stop facing forward. With this landing thus accomplished successfully, the gear was considered satisfactory and the B-50 mother ship flew the X-2 back to Buffalo for installation of its rocket engine.

It was assumed by everyone that the fuel system was safe to operate. After my explosion in the X-1D and Joe Cannon's fire in the X-1 No. 3 in November, 1951, both planes having low-pressure systems like the X-2, we had completely changed the propellant system to prevent any possible repetition in the newer airplane. The nitrogen tube bundles came out and were replaced by heavier cylinder tanks. This modification increased the weight of the X-2 some 800 pounds, resulting in a considerable sacrifice in performance, but we felt we had to make the airplane as safe to fly as was humanly possible.

Despite all our precautions, disaster struck again, this

time with tragic results. In May, 1953, on a captive test flight over Lake Ontario, another fire and explosion destroyed the X-2 in the bomb bay of the B-50. Skip Ziegler was in the bomb bay beside the rocket ship and was lost with the airplane, as was Frank Wolko, a Bell scanner in the mother ship. The big bomber was blown upward by the force of the blast and damaged so severely that it could not be used again, although Bell pilot Bill Leyshon and his crew brought it home. This meant another B-50 had to be modified, the second X-2 completed, and another rocket engine constructed. Through the combination of all these factors, together with serious doubts about the value of the program itself, more than a year elapsed before the X-2 flew again.

I still retained my early desire to fly this airplane. Despite the frustrating delays and the obvious hazards, it still challenged me. It is true the X-1A and X-1B were flying and I hoped to have another chance to set a record before the NACA got them. But they were not designed for the same speed, and I was well aware of their limitations. I wanted to do something no one else had done. It was the X-2 that offered the opportunity to fly still faster and explore farther into the unknown.

For this reason I went to see Colonel Hanes and General Holtoner early in 1954, when it appeared that the second X-2 was nearing completion, and told them I was highly interested in flying this airplane. I pointed out that Major Yeager, the only pilot with more rocket experience, would soon be leaving Edwards for a new assignment, and I was the next best qualified in rocket ships. With Ziegler dead, civilian pilots with comparable rocket experience were also unavailable. For these reasons, Colonel Hanes and General Holtoner agreed to let me fly at least the early tests on the new X-2, and I was officially designated the project pilot.

I went back to the Bell plant at Buffalo for about three weeks to familiarize myself with the engine and the new airplane. I studied the power plant and fuel systems painstakingly to understand their operation, making ground runs on the engine in the test bed at the factory, and learning the operating procedures by heart. The engine was not yet ready for actual flight tests. First I had to prove out the controls and flight characteristics of the new airplane. But the design was unchanged, so we anticipated no difficulty in our glide tests. The engine would be installed when these were completed, and in the meantime I took the opportunity to master every detail of the untried power plant.

In July, 1954, a new B-50 brought the X-2 to Edwards. Again it would fly with ballast instead of an engine. With the airplane came the devoted Bell engineers who would direct the test program—Stan Smith, the project engineer; Bob Lapp, his assistant; Jimmy Powell, flight test engineer; Jimmy Dunn, crew chief; and two score more engineers, specialists, and technicians. Two years before, I had been only an interested spectator; but now, as the project pilot, I was on the Bell team. I wore a military uniform but I was the pilot for a civilian test program. As a military man and officer, my first loyalty was to the Air Force. But I also came to know loyalty to these dedicated men and their problems. In this way, wearing two hats, I set forth on the X-2 flight test program.

I am a small man, 5 feet 7 inches tall and weighing 150 pounds, but even for me the X-2 cockpit was a very tight fit. I sat on the floor with the stick between my legs and my shoulders brushing the sides of the cockpit. Fully dressed with my parachute on, my helmet touched the top of the canopy, while I had to bend my legs to get my feet on the rudder bar. There was no room to turn sideways to reach the instruments, and to turn switches on the left side of the cockpit I had to use my right hand and vice versa.

Because of this limited cockpit space and the great number of instruments needed in the X-2, all panel instruments were built smaller than the standard models. For example, the electrical instruments were 1 inch in diameter, instead of the standard Air Force 4 inches. Counting the special instrumentation installed later for powered flights, the X-2 carried scores of separate instruments, filling every inch of space with dials, meters, and gauges. The list of instruments, switches, and controls to be checked before each flight totalled 127 different items.

On August 5, I made my first flight in the new X-2, which was to become the fastest and highest-flying airplane in the world. This was another glide flight, after air drop from the

B-50 mother ship, with empty fuel tanks and ballast instead of an engine. Under these conditions, the X-2 weighed about six and a half tons, only half its maximum gross weight fully loaded.

An Air Force pilot and crew flew the B-50 today for the first time. After talking it over with Bell, we agreed on a military crew. Bell was already supporting the airplane with nearly fifty people at Edwards, in addition to many more involved at Buffalo, and they all cost money. Air Force personnel could be assigned to the project without hiring people, and also they were on hand and immediately available for duty.

To fly the B-50 I selected one of my best test pilots, Captain Fitzhugh Fulton. Fitz was thoroughly experienced in bombers and fighters and knew the problems of both multi-engined and single-engine planes. He was also thoroughly familiar with the X-2 program, having worked with me on previous occasions, and he helped me set up the best techniques for climb and drop of the rocket ship.

We planned to drop at an altitude of 30,000 feet and a speed of 220 miles an hour indicated. At this speed and altitude, experience had proved the X-2 would fall free and I would have time for the necessary tests before I had to come down for the usual deadstick landing. Bell's contract called for a dive near Mach 1 and then pulling five G's to test structural integrity. Of course, the X-2 was built to withstand much greater forces.

Flying chase for me today was our most experienced rocket pilot, Major Charles Yeager. Chuck was my assistant in flight test now, waiting for overseas assignment, and as a result he was constantly available for advice and help. Because of his intimate knowledge of rocket planes, I was fortunate to be able to call on him, as his experience in the early X-1 program in many ways paralleled the work I was now beginning.

As we would not reach extreme altitudes or fly very fast without an engine, I did not equip myself with the pressure suit and pressure helmet that are essential in rocket ships. Instead I wore a standard warm-winter flying suit and the regulation crash helmet that I normally used in test work. I also wore the standard seat-type parachute, which I would need if something went wrong and I had to leave the airplane.

Not that I expected trouble. The X-2 was an honest air-plane and it liked to fly. We had established on early glide flights two years before that it was aerodynamically sound and responsive to its controls. I had also spent many hours in the X-2 cockpit and knew it by heart. I could hit the switches with my eyes closed and did not have to think about their location. This made it easier to fly the airplane, as I didn't worry about finding the right instruments when I needed them.

The purpose of this flight was to check the new hydraulic flight control system that was used in the new airplane and establish the best flight procedures prior to drop. This would be the first drop of the new X-2 from the mother ship. While it was identical with the airplane I had flown previously, it had not yet proved itself in the air, and until it did so we could not take anything for granted.

Captain Fulton dropped me at 30,000 feet without incident. I felt the airplane out both laterally and longitudinally to check out its handling characteristics and it responded very satisfactorily. Next I extended the landing gear and skid to test them. The green light in the instrument panel failed to light, indicating that the nose wheel had not fully extended, but when I pulled the nose of the airplane up sharply to shake the wheel down, the light came on, indicating it had extended and locked in position.

After testing the landing gear I fully lowered my wing flaps to test the flight characteristics. As I did so my air speed dropped sharply and I began losing altitude rapidly. To give myself a better glide ratio and more time to land I retracted the flaps halfway and entered the landing pattern.

I was set up to come in from the east on the dry lake bed, with a glide speed on the downwind leg of 220 miles an hour. At this time Major Yeager reported the whisker skid on my right wing had not extended and the nose wheel was cocked to the right 45 degrees. I immediately called the Bell radio truck on the ground and asked Jimmy Powell what would happen when I landed. He said the nose wheel should caster when it touched the ground and straighten out satisfactorily.

I came in like this, nose wheel turned to the right and one wing skid extended, and touched down about 170 miles an hour. The nose wheel touched the ground almost immediately.

As the nose of the airplane fell forward, the airplane veered sharply to the right. I had no brakes and the rudder was useless. The left wing-tip then struck the ground and the airplane turned full 90 degrees sideways. As it skidded crazily along the ground in this position, the left wing-tip hit the ground and threw the airplane completely around another 90 degrees. Still sliding along the ground at 100 miles an hour, the X-2 skidded backward across the lake bed until its momentum was exhausted. Realizing I was shaken up, Chuck said over the radio in his calm voice, "You're O.K. now, buddy." "Thanks a lot," I replied.

I pulled myself together and climbed out of the cockpit, badly shaken. At any moment I had expected the careening airplane to cartwheel over on its back with me underneath it. The X-2 was not badly damaged, but both wing tips were bent and scarred and the nose wheel strut was bent and wedged up in the wheel well. As a result of this damage, Bell took the X-2 back to Buffalo. It could not fly again until the damage was repaired and as the new Curtiss-Wright rocket engine was finally nearing completion, we decided to install the engine while we repaired the airplane.

As things turned out, our trip to Buffalo was unnecessary. Delays in the engine installation made it impossible to wait for the power plant to finish the gear tests. We already had lost six months without getting the engine. Unable to wait any longer, Bell brought the X-2 out to Edwards again in February, 1955, for the second glide flight of this airplane.

A new test was scheduled for this flight, intended to find the best techniques for topping off the liquid oxygen from the mother airplane. Ernie Kreutinger, the Bell top-off man in the B-50, would accompany Bill Fleming, the X-2 panel operator on this flight, and with them I would practice the best method for refilling the X-2 lox tanks to replace the essential oxydizer as it constantly boiled away during the slow climb. I would also test the best procedures for dumping the lox and water alcohol in the event my engine failed to start. After jettisoning the fuel, I would then come back down and test the landing gear.

It was our feeling that the nose wheel was the chief source of trouble. As a result, we had revised the wheel fork to reduce the amount it could turn or caster. In this way we hoped to prevent it from turning and wedging itself in the wheel well again, even if it failed to extend and lock in position. If we could do this, we believed the airplane would slide in a straight line on the ground and avoid further damage.

We took off at 7:30 A.M. on March 8 and climbed to altitude, where we tested the lox top-off procedures. As they appeared satisfactory, I then prepared to test the procedures for jettisoning the propellants. It was quickly apparent that they were inadequate and even dangerous.

The X-2 had been designed to empty its fuel tanks in sequence to maintain longitudinal balance of the airplane and keep its center of gravity fairly constant. In powered flight the rocket engine would burn fuel at the rate of 600 gallons or nearly two tons a minute; in event of power failure, I could not hope to land unless I dumped it. Even with half-empty tanks the sheer weight of the propellants would push touch-down speed of the X-2 to about 250 miles an hour, above permissible limits; and in any event the landing gear was not stressed to take the load. But in order to jettison, the lox tanks had to empty at the same rate to keep the center of gravity from shifting, and we now discovered that the lox tanks did not jettison evenly.

Nor did they empty fast enough. The best we could do was ten minutes to get them both dry. Later we corrected this problem by installing 3-inch jettison tubes, which reduced jettison time to about two minutes. We also modified the system to make sure the tanks emptied evenly. But today we had other things to worry about, particularly the inevitable deadstick landing. When my fuel tanks were empty I closed and locked the cockpit canopy and Fleming and Kreutinger climbed back into the B-50. With a last look at my instruments I signaled Captain Fulton that I was ready and he dropped me.

I immediately dove the airplane to pick up airspeed, then pulled the nose up to approach stall in a clean configuration with gear and flaps up. At 160 miles an hour the airframe began to buffet. As I felt the stall warning I pushed over and recovered flying speed, then dropped the gear and flaps.

In this dirty configuration I made stick pulses at 190 miles an hour, followed by another stall approach down to 140.

Then I saw that I was again sinking too fast with flaps fully extended and retracted them halfway.

Today I had again set up my landing pattern to the west. I touched down about 160 miles an hour and the nose wheel made contact with the ground without difficulty. The X-2 was sliding in a fairly straight line across the lake bed, turning a little to the left but under control, when it crossed over an oil strip marking the runway boundary. As it did so I lost control completely. The airplane skidded violently to the left, then to the right, and came to a halt on its right wing tip. Once more I crawled out of the cockpit badly shaken by my experience. However, there was only minor damage to the airplane this time, and I was inclined to blame it on the runway marker.

To be on the safe side, Bell increased the pressure of the whisker skids on the ground by 50 per cent, giving them each 800 pounds per square inch of footprint pressure. With this additional support, Stan Smith and Bob Lapp felt the skids would have a better stabilizing effect and that more positive lateral control would be forthcoming.

These changes were made, and four weeks later I took the X-2 up for its third glide flight. The date was April 2. The purpose of this flight was to test the stall and landing characteristics of the airplane with leading edge flaps retracted, the first time we had flown it in this configuration. We also wanted to check on the new whisker skid modifications.

Once more Captain Fulton dropped me from the B-50 at 30,000 feet and I felt out the airplane. As I retracted the leading edge flaps it buffeted severely and I extended them again immediately. They remained extended during my let-down until I landed, when I retracted them again.

As I did so, the nose of the airplane pitched forward violently on the ground and the plane began rolling from side to side in a sickening oscillating motion. The more I tried to stop it the worse it became. Finding myself completely out of phase with the rolling motion, I let go of the control stick entirely and grasped the crash bar with both hands, hoping the airplane would straighten itself out. As I did so it yawed violently to the right and slammed to a stop turned fully sideways.

Despite the nylon straps that held me in my seat, the sudden deceleration hurled me against the side of the cockpit, and for one awful second I felt the X-2 start to tip over. Then somehow it settled back again on the desert floor, its wild energy spent, and I relaxed my desperate grip on the iron bar in front of me. Completely unnerved by my narrow escape from disaster, this time I was shaken so badly I was ready to quit.

It was after this flight that I told the Bell company they would have to find a permanent solution to the landing gear problem on the X-2 before it would fly again.

11

Mach 2.5

As a result of my bitter complaints and the obvious hazards involved to the airplane and the pilot, a fresh attempt was made to improve the landing gear on the X-2. The airplane was flown back to the Bell company plant at Buffalo, New York, in the B-50 mother ship, and a modification program got under way.

Our first step was a series of meetings to analyze the problem and suggest solutions. Bell company engineers, landing gear experts from the Wright Field aircraft laboratory, and people from Edwards, including myself, had many meetings in an attempt to find out why the landing gear system was not operating properly. We ran many checks and tests on scale models and on the actual airplane. Out of these tests and conferences came design changes that solved the problem.

The most important change was reduction in the stroke, or length, of the hydraulic piston on the main landing skid. We reduced its length by half, cutting the landing gear strut from 30 to 15 inches fully extended. This also lowered the vertical center of gravity of the airplane by putting it closer to the ground. I had always felt that the X-2 sat too high on the skid, which was a destabilizing influence on lateral-directional control, and by placing the airplane lower, I could better maintain control on the ground.

In another change, the nose wheel was modified to reduce the friction in the castering system, which permitted it to turn more easily upon contact with the ground. Finally, we increased the width of the main landing skid from 12 to 21 inches to increase lateral stability. The new skid was actually wider than the bottom of the fuselage and dirtied up the airplane considerably by increasing air resistance. However, it was primarily an extra precaution, and we were prepared to replace it with the original 12-inch skid if I found that the extra width was unnecessary.

After many tests of scale models of the new landing gear configuration, I felt satisfied with the modifications and I was willing to make another flight to check out the installation. The Curtiss-Wright rocket engine for which we had been waiting also became available at this time and was installed in the airplane at Buffalo. Early in October we returned to Edwards Air Force Base and preparations got under way for the first powered flight of the X-2.

There was some doubt about attempting a powered flight on the airplane before we checked out the new landing gear system, but we did so because of the time problem. Time was running out for this airplane. The X-2 project was already ten years old and had not yet produced any worthwhile results. Many millions of dollars had been spent with no apparent return on the investment. At the same time, newer aircraft would soon be flying which could provide data on high-speed flight. Because of this time problem and the other factors involved, we had been given a deadline beyond which the X-2 would not be flown at all—December 31, less than three months away. If the X-2 could not be flown by the end of the year, the project would be abandoned.

In these circumstances, we perhaps took risks that would not normally be taken. We flew an untried power plant and an untried landing gear system simultaneously because we could not afford to wait to test them separately. We naturally assumed that we would have to make changes in the power plant, which would take still more time. Had we conducted the gear tests first and damaged the airplane on landing, the engine information would have been denied us until a later date; but by flying the engine as soon as possible, we could get performance data and go ahead with any power plant modifications that might be needed, even though the airplane cracked up on landing. As a matter of fact, we were prepared to make further changes on both the landing gear and the engine at the same time.

That is why we combined both tests on my next flight. To us this was the culmination of ten long years of work and hardship. Two lives and two airplanes had already been sacrificed in the X-2 project. Costs had increased far beyond original estimates. Now, in the few weeks remaining out of the time allotted us, we had our last chance to redeem the work of years.

There were other problems involved too. Wind tunnel studies had indicated the possibility of a little trouble in the airplane during transonic flight. As a result, we wanted to approach this area very cautiously and investigate it thoroughly before going into a higher speed regime.

On the first powered flight I planned to turn on the small rocket chamber at low thrust, climb to altitude, then make some maneuvers to check out the controls under operating conditions. After that I would increase my speed very slowly, while at the same time my chase pilot would observe the airplane very closely from the outside. If I got into the trouble area that was anticipated, we would compare notes on the situation as we found it, and I would decide at that time whether to discontinue the flight. If the buffet was not severe I planned to increase my speed beyond Mach 1.

The flight was called for October 25. Stu Childs, who was chief of my fighter branch at Edwards, was flying chase today in an F-100 jet fighter, accompanied by photographers in F-86 and T-33 photo planes. Fitzhugh Fulton again was flying the B-50 mother ship. A larger crowd than usual gathered on the flight line for my take-off, including some fifty Bell company personnel. This was the first time the new engine had ever been flown in this airplane and its many new features made it of special interest. It was also the first time that a rocket engine with a throttle had been flown in this country. In addition, the concept of a gas generator to be used as a pressure source for the fuel system was still new. It was the engine that worried me most because I could not depend on it to keep running. In ground tests it had shown a dangerous tendency to stop unexpectedly at any time.

Shortly after we took off in the B-50, I entered the X-2 cockpit at an altitude of 2,000 or 3,000 feet. We had found on previous flights that I must make an early entry, in order to be strapped in and connected up before reaching 10,000

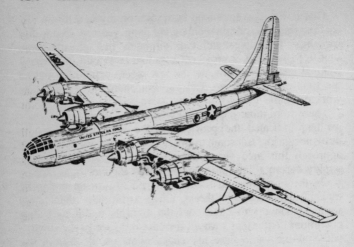

B-50

feet. The men helping me were working without oxygen, which they needed at higher altitudes.

John Wray, who handled flying equipment for our test pilots, was my pressure suit officer today. He accompanied me in the B-50 and helped me struggle into my pressure suit and pressure helmet. Then he crawled down the ladder after me to the X-2 and helped me get settled in place for the flight. My pressure suit was connected to the X-2 oxygen system and my radio headset to the X-2 radio cord. Then I was strapped down very securely in the little cockpit, with a crotch strap around my legs in addition to a waist belt and shoulder harness.

Ernie Kreutinger from Bell was top-off man for the X-2 fuel system. It was his responsibility as the B-50 climbed to altitude to refill the liquid oxygen that constantly boiled off from the rocket ship, giving me full fuel tanks when the X-2 began independent flight. In the meantime Ernie helped Captain Wray strap me in the cockpit, and after I was ready to go, Wray helped him put the canopy securely in place.

As they climbed back into the B-50 bomb bay I began my long check of the X-2 controls and instruments. It was at this point that I noticed that my nitrogen source pressure was leaking excessively. I was extremely reluctant to say anything about it at first, hoping it was temporary. Everyone concerned with the flight had worked himself up to a high state of anticipation, and I knew a decision to abort at this point would be a terrible disappointment.

Finally I called in Bill Fleming over the radio, the Bell engineer in the B-50 handling the X-2 operating panel, and tried to come up with a solution to the problem. When this failed I called in Jimmy Powell, the flight test engineer, in the Bell radio truck on the ground. He was also reluctant to abandon the powered flight that we had all waited for so long; but we agreed that without a pressure source to operate the fuel system we could not attempt a powered flight.

So I jettisoned the liquid oxygen and water alcohol in the X-2, and Captain Fulton dropped me at 220 miles an hour at 32,000 feet. Gliding the airplane, I made some pullups and roll checks at speeds from 200 to 320 miles an hour, noting a slight airframe buffet that increased with the speed of the airplane. However, Major Childs was observing me from his F-100 chase plane, and reported that neither ailerons nor rudder were buffeting visibly.

Now it was time to land with the modified main skid and nose wheel that had caused me so many anxious moments on previous flights. At 10,000 feet I extended the main skid and lowered my wing flaps on the leading and trailing edges of the X-2's sweptback wings. Turning from base leg to final approach my air speed dropped sharply, and I touched down about 175 miles an hour.

The touchdown on the main skid was quite gentle. After sliding along for 500 feet, the nose of the X-2 pitched down and the nose wheel touched the ground. I noticed with great relief that the airplane continued to move across the lake bed in a fairly straight line. There was no lateral movement during the landing roll, but from 60 miles an hour down to stop the plane moved to the right directionally a few degrees.

Of course I held on to the crash bar with both hands, prepared for a possible repetition of my previous experiences, and in my anxiety I even forgot to retract my flaps. Because the landing roll was fairly straight, however, this did no damage. As my dusty slide along the desert floor continued with nothing worse than the shock and bump of a normal landing, I began to relax. Then I took one hand off the crash bar and applied left aileron and right rudder to maintain directional control. It had no visible effect on the slight yaw I had noticed previously but the angle did not increase.

As Jimmy Powell ran up to greet me I saw that he was grinning. I was too. We knew the landing gear problem was licked, and this was a major consolation for the failure to start the engine. The lowered main skid on the X-2, which brought it nearly a foot closer to the ground, had apparently ended the danger of a skidding airplane cartwheeling sideways out of control. In fact, with the lower center of gravity we now had on the airplane, we planned to go back to the original 12-inch skid on the next flight.

After fixing the leak in nitrogen source pressure and running several engine tests on the ground to bring it up to operating condition, I took the X-2 up again on November 16 for another attempt at powered flight.

The purpose of the flight was to attempt rocket power and check handling characteristics of the X-2 at moderately high Mach numbers, not to exceed Mach 1.5. Again everyone connected with the project was in a state of suspense and anticipation. The climb to altitude was normal and I dropped from the B-50 at a speed of 255 miles an hour at 30,000 feet.

The drop was more abrupt than usual, as the airplane carried a full load of fuel at drop for the first time. Total gross weight including fuel was over 25,000 pounds—twice as heavy as the empty configuration. With this high gross weight I thought it possible the X-2 might stall out before I could get the engine started, and I was more tense than usual. But the drop was satisfactory, and as I started the small rocket chamber the X-2 began flying under its own power for the first time.

Except for a slight amount of airframe buffet, which I could not identify, the airplane handled easily. I put the nose down in a shallow dive to increase speed to Mach .8, then pulled it up in a moderate climb. Stu Childs, who was flying chase for me in the F-100, moved in close and made a visual inspection of the control surfaces. I then increased speed up to Mach .9 and Major Childs immediately reported a buffet in the horizontal stabilizer.

I cut the engine to stop the buffet, and speed decreased to Mach .8. Then I started the small chamber again and once more began climbing and accelerating. Still chasing me at Mach .95, just under the speed of sound, Childs reported horizontal stabilizer buffet again at 45,000 feet. However, it was not severe enough for me to feel it.

A third time I went through the same procedure in an effort to pinpoint the disturbance on the control surfaces—cut the engine, bleed off speed to Mach .8, then restart the small chamber and pick up speed again. As I did so the rocket engine coughed convulsively and quit cold. I tried once more to start it but without success, so I jettisoned my remaining fuel and came on home.

Inspection of the aircraft revealed an external fire in the rocket engine compartment. Fuel from the dump valve had sucked up in the tail of the airplane and ignited from the hot chamber. The rudder and airframe were both severely scorched before the fire burnt itself out. Had it continued for any length of time I probably would have lost stabilizer control, with consequent loss and destruction of the airplane.

The fire damage had to be repaired, delaying further flights for several days, and we also had to make some engine modifications. At about the same time, the X-1A caught fire and exploded in the B-50 mother ship, much the same as in my accident in the X-1D and the explosion that killed Skip Ziegler in the other X-2. As a result of these two fires, the remaining X-2 was grounded several months for major changes in the lox tank and propellant system, and it was March, 1956, before I was able to fly it again.

On March 26 I made my second powered flight, reaching a speed of Mach .91. On April 25 I pushed this up to Mach 1.4 and on May 1 to Mach 1.5. While this was well below my top speed of Mach 2.3 in the X-1B, set two years previously, still it represented a healthy growth for the new plane. Not only were we learning more about its flight characteristics and power plant, but we were also establishing the methods and techniques needed to reach still higher altitudes and speeds. Although there was doubt that the X-2 would ever reach its design speed, we decided to continue the tests to see how close we could come to this figure. On May 11 I pushed the speed up a little higher to Mach 1.8, and eleven days later, on May 22, reached a speed never before flown by man.

This was an all-out flight to see exactly what the X-2 could do in its present configuration. Another early take-off was scheduled, when winds were calm and other flying activity was at a minimum. The ground crew came in at 3 A.M. to check and calibrate the instrumentation for the flight and load the volatile and highly hazardous propellants in the airplane. For this flight, the X-2 again carried a full load of fuel—900 gallons of liquid oxygen and 850 to 900 gallons of water alcohol. Together they weighed nearly 13,000 pounds—more than the empty weight of the airplane. The rate of burn-out, of course, would depend on the amount of thrust I used. At full power the fuel would last only seconds.

I had an early breakfast with Avis, looked in at the sleeping children, then drove to the flight line in the old Model A Ford that had seen so many flights in rocket ships. Dawn came sooner now and the desert sunrise was already breaking in the eastern sky. Stu Childs was on hand to fly chase for me again, accompanied by Captain Iven Kincheloe and Captain Milburn Apt. Fitz Fulton was flying the B-50, with the normal complement of Bell personnel to help him in the airplane and monitor the flight on the ground.

Although the time was late May, I was wearing winter underwear under my pressure suit, with a heavy flying suit on top to keep me warm. I was going to altitudes today where air temperatures were 60 degrees below zero. Under my heavy flying boots were two pairs of socks, one silk and one heavy wool. I also wore two pairs of gloves, one silk and one leather, to keep my hands from freezing in the unheated plane.

At 30,000 feet Captain Fulton bent the B-50 over and dropped me at 250 miles an hour. Immediately after drop I started the large rocket chamber and rounded out to level flight. Then I applied full power and began my climb.

I realized at once that the X-2 was accelerating very rapidly— much too fast for me to hold it down. Although my climb angle was very steep, the minimum speed I could maintain was 370 miles an hour. I held this climb speed to 55,000 feet, where I began my push-over.

As the X-2 leveled out toward horizontal flight it picked up speed noticeably and passed Mach 2—twice the speed of sound. This was a new record for the airplane and it was still accelerating. At 60,000 feet I was straight and level and continued my push-over. At 57,000 feet I was in a shallow dive and speed was Mach 2.5. Hurtling me through space just under 1,600 miles an hour, the rocket engine exhausted its fuel supply and shut down.

After rocket shutdown, I noted that the X-2 was very stable both laterally and directionally. There was a slight undamped pitching oscillation after I pulsed the stabilizer. However, this pitching moment was controllable. Aileron effectiveness decreased but rate of response to aileron was excellent.

Gliding the airplane now, I turned back toward the dry lake bed 10 miles below me. My thoughts and emotions were mixed elation and concern. I was happy to know that I had broken my own speed record in the X-1B by approximately 100 miles an hour and also the X-1A record by about 50 miles an hour, although this was an insignificant number. I also believed the X-2 was capable of even higher speeds, but only under ideal conditions.

This would mean dropping from a higher altitude, maintaining a better climb schedule and perhaps diving at a steeper angle after push-over. More important, some way had to be found to increase rocket time, as every additional second of power meant many more miles an hour. This was possible, but it would take time. And time was my major problem.

Time was my problem because I was scheduled to leave Edwards for a new assignment. It was ten years now since I'd begun testing planes for the Air Force. Four years at Wright Field and then six years at Edwards—much longer than a military man ever stays in one assignment. I had been lucky, getting what I wanted to do most—test airplanes—and doing it for ten rewarding years. But time was up now.

In comparison with other Air Force officers of comparable grade and service, the scope of my military career to date was very narrow. Now I had a new assignment to the Armed Forces Staff College at Norfolk, Virginia—a chance to broaden my experience and knowledge and an opportunity to learn new things and exchange ideas with other services. After school I ought to go overseas again; in ten years most officers had been over at least once, some two or three times. I was on orders to leave for Norfolk July 15, and I knew it was time to go. Except for the X-2, I was almost ready to leave. It was time to move on.

Except for the X-2. That was the part I hated—leaving the X-2 and all it had come to mean to me over the years I'd lived and worked with this airplane. Starting back in 1949, when I first stumbled across it in the Bell factory at Buffalo; ever since 1952, when I made a glide flight in the first airplane, and through the past fifteen months of gliding and flying the X-2, I had lived with it for many years, through all its growing pains, until it was more or less a part of me.

Avis didn't like it at all; it frightened her. Perhaps it scared me a little too, but it was a challenge and it gave me a thrill. Maybe that was why I liked it—because it went fast. Yes, that was it; I knew it could go even faster, and it was a challenge to do more. We could put rocket extenders on the rocket tubes to increase thrust; and we could shorten the fuel probes in the fuel tanks to give us more rocket time. With these modifications, I knew the X-2 would go even faster than Mach 2.5. But installing rocket extenders and new fuel probes would take time. And I didn't have much time.

Meanwhile I recommended that no more high-speed flights be attempted until these modifications were completed. The rocket extenders were being ground-tested at the Curtiss-Wright plant in New Jersey and would be delayed two or three weeks; shorter fuel probes could be installed at Edwards, so they were less of a problem. While we were waiting for these changes, I checked out the new pilot who would fly the X-2 after I had gone.

I selected Captain Iven Kincheloe and Captain Milburn Apt, both of them test pilots with superior skills and qualifications. Kincheloe was selected as my first alternate. He was a Korea jet ace, a graduate of the Empire Test Pilot School in England, and one of the finest test pilots in my command. His flying ability was outstanding and his attitude beyond reproach.

Captain Apt had been a flight test engineer at Wright Field

and then attended the Edwards test pilot school. He too had shown outstanding attitude and ability, and was my choice for second alternate X-2 pilot. If I did not have time to complete the high-speed tests on this airplane, Kincheloe would finish the speed runs and Apt would try for the altitude record. However, time was limited for them too, as the Air Force was committed to completing its tests by November 1 and turning the X-2 over to NACA for stability testing.

I checked Kincheloe out in the airplane on May 25. I gave him a thorough cockpit check before take-off and then flew chase for him. He attained supersonic speed and made a fairly decent landing. Through press of other duties, Apt was not checked out at this time, but we planned to do this at a later date. In the meantime, he continued working with me on the project, and was well acquainted with the airplane.

On my last flight, at a top speed of Mach 2.5, we had gained valuable new information on the effects of thermal heating as well as stability and control. For the time duration of this flight we had found that heating resulting from air friction on the fuselage at that speed and altitude was not a problem of any significance. We also knew the airplane could be controlled. Now we wanted to expand the speed/altitude envelope still further to determine if heat would be a problem at speeds above Mach 2.5. We also wanted to find out if the airplane was controllable at higher Mach numbers.

The flight plan for the next high-speed flight called for climb to maximum altitude in the B-50 before drop, then turn on full power in both rocket chambers immediately after drop and climb until becoming supersonic. Then attempt to maintain a climb speed of Mach 1.1 to 1.2 to 60,000 feet, where I would start a slow pushover and accelerate to the maximum speed possible with fuel available.

It was the end of June, a full month of fretting and waiting, before the new rocket extenders arrived at Edwards, and another week before they were installed and tested. I was still on orders to leave July 15. I had already turned over most of my administrative duties to Danny Grubaugh, my assistant, and he was now performing the paper work that normally occupied much of my time. As a result, I felt more or less like a fish out of water, waiting for one more flight and wondering if the X-2 would be ready in time.

Because of many long hours of overtime work by NACA and Bell company personnel, the airplane was once more in operating condition on July 12. Counting Kincheloe's check flight, this would be the eighth powered flight of the X-2. We had done everything we knew to make it a successful one. The airplane was cleaned and waxed by hand to reduce air resistance to a minimum. The water-alcohol was cold-soaked in liquid oxygen to reduce its volume and thus get a few more gallons into the fuel tanks. The probes had been shortened to drain the last drop of fuel out of them, and the rocket extenders were installed and working satisfactorily.

The morning of the flight I was in a strange state of anticipation, feeling this would be my last flight in the X-2. Captain Fulton dropped me at 250 miles an hour indicated. I gave the airplane full throttle and started my climb, both rocket chambers firing and hurling me skyward like the steel tip on a giant arrow.

The X-2 accelerated very rapidly. I attempted to hold the proper climb schedule, cradling the control stick in my arms and bracing my feet against the rudder bars to strengthen my grip. But climbing as it was on maximum power, the rocket ship was being flung nearly straight up by the fiery force of its propellants, and the steep climb angle made longitudinal control difficult, if not impossible.

I fought the controls with every nerve and muscle, my whole body shaking as the battering wind forces shook the careening airplane in its headlong flight. In front of me on the instrument panel, the black needle in the unfeeling Machmeter reached and then passed the speed of sound. Noise was again behind me, except for the whistling air that sighed and sang its strange music over the rushing plane. Outside I saw sunlight without color, like water or crystal, except above me at the zenith where the sky stretched deep purple across the arch of space.

As the altimeter needle touched 60,000 feet, I squared my shoulders painfully against the steel couch I leaned on and pushed the control stick away from me, very slowly, very deliberately, like a man aiming a gun or a surgeon moving his knife. I could feel the pressure upward against my shoulder harness as the airplane responded to the controls and its nose moved down perceptibly toward level flight.

I held forward pressure on the stick, pushing over and accelerating simultaneously. Centrifugal force still flung the airplane upward, and I was fighting this force with the control surfaces that deflected the X-2 toward a level flight path. As my stick pressure increased there was a sudden jerk forward against my shoulder harness as the airplane decelerated. I knew from the jerk and a glance at the instrument panel that my rocket engine had stopped.

Aware that I had a rocket shutdown, my feeling was one of frustration and bewilderment. What could have gone wrong this time? I thought of the gas generator that turned the fuel turbine pump. In ground runs recently there had been trouble with generator overtemperature, causing automatic shutdown. Had this happened again? The airplane was rigged to be very safe—almost too safe, I thought—so far as overtemperatures, overpressures, and other fire warnings were concerned. We had a lot of trouble with false fire indications, interrupting engine run-ups, and I felt we should have taken out some of these so-called safety devices and made the airplane a little safer to fly.

Whatever the reason, she quit dead at Mach 1.5, and my last chance to set a new speed record was gone. After all the work and waiting that had gone into this flight, I felt deep remorse and heartbreak, not only for myself but for all those others who had worked so hard and long. I hesitated a few seconds before breaking radio silence, keenly aware of the high degree of anticipation with which they waited for word from me, and knowing how much they would be disappointed.

However, I had to tell them sometime, so with great reluctance I called in the radio truck at the air base to report my engine had just quit. I didn't know why. Yes, everything was O.K. I was returning to land. There was a moment of silence, and I could picture them shaking their heads and wondering what happened. And after that the feeling that they had worked so hard, and again the same weary question in the minds of everyone: "What could have gone wrong this time?"

That was what they thought, but they didn't say it. All they said was, "O.K., fine. Glad everything's all right. Come on in and land. We'll give it another try." Only this time there wouldn't be another try. This time I was on my way to another assignment—to fly a desk instead of the world's fastest airplane. This was the last time.

Although there was still fuel in my tanks, I did not jettison it, bringing it back to measure it and find out if the shortened fuel probes had worked successfully. On landing this was the first thing we checked. We found 250 gallons of fuel remaining—and we also found out why the rocket engine had stopped running.

I had overcontrolled. After going supersonic and starting to round out for the speed run, I put negative G on the airplane. I overcontrolled longitudinally, and during the overcontrolling—pushing down to a negative G—I uncovered the fuel probes that we had made shorter to scrub the tanks. The fuel in the final tank, forced to the top by the motion of the airplane, actuated the electrical sensing devices in the probe, and mistakenly sensing that the fuel was exhausted, it shut off the valves in every cell, bypassing those that had fuel left in them.

It was easy to fix this problem. We could modify the probe system with a timing relay, giving a 5-second delay before the valves would close. If the pilot subjected the airplane to a negative G on future flights and uncovered the probes, the sensing element would wait 5 seconds, by which time he probably would come back to a positive G and fuel would cover the probes again. On the other hand, if the cell was really empty, the probes would remain uncovered and after the 5 seconds were up the valves would close.

I didn't know what to do. We discussed the problems and the Bell people wanted me to get another flight. By working twenty-four hours a day they said they could have the airplane ready to fly again in two or three days. Of course I could not ask them to work like that and said so. Then I discussed the situation with Colonel Hanes and he suggested I stay over a few extra days if necessary. This made me feel better, as it took the pressure off everybody, and I agreed. With that the Bell boys went back to work to fix the X-2 once more, to give me one more flight.

The one-week time extension I planned on stretched out to eleven days. Although the timing relay was installed on schedule, unforeseen circumstances brought other delays. After changing the fuel probes, we discovered an alcohol leak and took two days to fix it. No sooner was this done than we discovered a liquid oxygen leak. We tried unsuccessfully to find this leak, finally changing the large rocket chamber before it was corrected.

At this point a new alcohol leak developed and had to be repaired. Then we found another oxygen leak. Again we changed the large rocket chamber and tested it. This time the ground test of the engine was successful, as we had neither a liquid oxygen leak nor a water alcohol leak. That was Sunday, July 22. Keeping our fingers crossed, another flight was called for the next morning.

12

1,900 Miles an Hour

The purpose of the ninth powered flight of the Bell X-2 rocket plane was to expand the speed/altitude envelope to a point approaching Mach 3, in order to evaluate the handling and stability characteristics of the airplane and the air friction temperatures encountered at extreme Mach numbers. This would be faster than man had ever flown before. We were shooting for three times the speed of sound, which is nearly 2,300 miles an hour at sea level. Of course, my true air speed would not be that high where I was flying as the speed of sound decreases with altitude.

I was well aware of what I was getting into, and thoroughly understood the limits I would face. Before this flight, as I had on previous tests, I had flown the GEDA machine, a Goodyear electronic digital analyzer, which could predict actual flight conditions based on the information we gave it. We had fed in the various stability parameters at anticipated Mach numbers and altitudes and assimilated these with the control stick, and had noted that under certain conditions the airplane would ''uncork'' and go out of control.

For example, if I pulsed the ailerons too much—moved them too far—at the higher Mach numbers, the X-2 would become uncontrollable. Or if I made too tight a turn at high speeds, GEDA would show me going out of control. The high-speed flight station of the National Advisory Committee for Aeronautics at Edwards Air Force Base, which furnished us much of the advice and guidance on X-2 instrumentation, had extrapolated previous flight data and forecast the stability limits of the airplane. They told me frankly what the dangers were on future flights and I had to stay within these limits. I followed directions and that is why I am here today.

Preparation for the flight began on Sunday. The water alcohol was cooled to zero degrees Fahrenheit in order to condense it and get the maximum fuel load on board. The Bell ground crew and technicians completed preflight inspection of the aircraft and engine, after which NACA personnel installed high-speed flight instrumentation and established zeroes. New batteries were installed and then the X-2 was mated to its B-50 mother ship in preparation for a dawn take-off the following morning.

Instrumentation included all the pressure pickups that were needed to make a complete record of the flight. This included the rocket chambers, the fuel and lox tanks, the intake and exit ports of the gas generator, and the intake and exhaust for the turbine pump. Strain gauge pickups were installed on the rudder, ailerons, and stabilizer to measure the forces that I would apply to these control surfaces. We also installed position pickups on the control stick, the rudder, and the control surfaces to determine the position of all controls and their surfaces at all times during the flight.

A yaw meter would measure the degree of yaw of the airplane in flight. Another instrument measured the angle of attack. Roll-and-bank and acceleration instruments gave us a record of acceleration in all directions—fore and aft, lateral and longitudinal. The X-2 also carried a small very-high-frequency radio transmitter that I would use to report my progress verbally, with a recording device on the ground to take down my comments.

Because I expected to run into high-speed heating on this flight, we had installed surface temperature pickup gauges to measure the air friction temperatures. We had also painted the airplane with stripes of heat-resistant paint. They were various bright colors, each color designed to withstand a specific temperature before it melted, and the nose and leading edges of the X-2 looked like a rainbow. As each color melted and started to run, we could estimate the approximate temperature encountered on that part of the airplane.

A radar homing beacon was installed to enable the NACA calibrated radar station at the main base to follow my flight.

Both NACA and the Air Force radar would track me, giving my speed and altitude as a check against my flight instruments. Because they sometimes lost me, Askania would also track me as a check against the radar. This was a big camera like a reflecting telescope, using theodolite tracking, which would observe and record my speed and altitude throughout the flight.

As on previous tests, this flight was a three-way project of Bell, NACA, and the Air Force. Bell and the Air Force were primarily interested in performance at high speeds, while NACA was more interested in stability characteristics. The Air Force funded the airplane—that is, paid the bill—and furnished the facilities; Bell and NACA ran the flights.

Bob Lapp, the X-2 project engineer at Bell, was in over-all charge and laid out the general program. Jimmy Powell, the flight test engineer, called the signals and did the detailed planning. Walt Williams of NACA furnished much of the detail analysis necessary to planning and programming, and Air Force personnel supplemented the required engineering services.

At 4 A.M. on the flight line at South Base Monday morning, Jimmy Dunn, the X-2 crew chief, signaled his ground crew to begin pumping six tons of water alcohol and liquid oxygen into the waiting rocket ship. Working in predawn darkness, the sleepy men moved silently about the airplane, making it ready for another assault against space.

It was 5 A.M. when the alarm clock roused me from my sleep. The first light of morning was creeping above the eastern desert, and looking out the window to check the weather, I saw with concern that the sky was overcast. The X-2 did not have the required instruments, so I could not attempt a deadstick landing through clouds. I had built myself up mentally in preparation for this flight and did not relish the prospect of weather forcing us to cancel it.

I immediately telephoned the weather officer at the base for a prediction of cloud cover at take-off time. He forecast three to four-tenths cover at 7 A.M., which would not be a problem, and as I hung up and began to dress I felt greatly relieved.

For breakfast I had an eggnog and a piece of toast. I was not hungry and couldn't eat more. After breakfast I went in to see the children but they were still asleep. Avis came out on the porch with me and I kissed her good-by. "Wish me luck," I said. She was under the same pressure I was, having delayed our departure more than a week to get this flight off, and both of us were a little tense. She clung to me a moment, then straightened up and smiled. "I wish you all the luck and love in the world," she said.

I drove to the flight line to check on the airplane, then continued to my office to dress for the flight. The other pilots were already there waiting for me—Captain Fulton, the B-50 pilot, and the three chase pilots, Major Childs, Captain Kincheloe, and Captain Apt. Captain Wray had my pressure suit laid out and helped me put it on. I studied my preflight check list a few minutes, then drove back to the flight line for a 6:30 take-off.

Take-off was delayed about fifteen minutes, so I stood around with the other pilots and the Bell people, talking and watching them finish fueling. I talked to Bob Lapp and went over the flight plan again with Jimmy Powell. I asked Jimmy Dunn about the airplane and if there was anything to watch out for. But mostly we just stood around and waited, kidding back and forth, as there was more than the usual amount of tension in the air and we were all trying not to show it.

At 6:45 Jimmy Powell called the B-50 crew to board the aircraft and activity began to increase. I zipped up my pressure suit and put on my heavy flying suit over it. One last handshake with the men remaining behind, and I got in the B-50 and went forward up in the nose to the bombardier's position, which I usually occupied during the take-off run.

We taxied out and received tower clearance, and less than a minute later were air-borne. After gear and flaps came up I went back in the B-50 and sat down near the X-2 control panel with Bill Fleming, the Bell panel engineer. Captain Wray helped me adjust my pressure helmet and strapped it down. Then he connected my bail-out bottle to the pressure suit and strapped on my parachute. I took a last look around the bomb bay and proceeded to enter the X-2.

Captain Wray and Ernie Kreutinger, the Bell top-off man in the B-50, followed me down and helped strap me in the cockpit. I was keenly aware that they were probably doing this for the last time. After I was strapped in and connected to the oxygen and radio outlets, I checked in over the radio with

Fulton in the B-50 and Jimmy Powell on the ground. The radio checked O.K. so I went to the other items still remaining on my preflight check list—turning on the various circuit breakers, checking hydraulic pressures and flight controls, and turning on my oxygen system.

Sunlight was now flooding the B-50 and the X-2 as we climbed laboriously upward, circling slowly in a heavy spiral that would take us to drop altitude six miles above the ground. But below us daylight had not yet reached the desert where the little cavalcade of vehicles moved in semi-darkness across the lake bed to take up its position at the south end of the lake. It moved slowly through the main gate and across the hard-packed ground, the radio truck leading the way, followed by eight or nine other vehicles carrying the fifty-odd men and women who would follow the news of my flight and meet me when I landed. Silently now, listening for any word from the B-50, they regrouped themselves half a mile off the landing strip where I would come down, and waited.

Up in the X-2, Wray and Kreutinger carefully slid the heavy plate-glass canopy into position and I locked it from the inside, sealing the cockpit against the outside world until I was once more back on earth. Despite myself, I felt a pang of loneliness and isolation. When they climbed back into the B-50 and moved out of sight in the bomber, I was aware that I would not see a human being again until I was on the ground.

We were above the clouds now, still climbing, but the overcast had increased. Weather reported by radio that cloud cover was four to eight-tenths overcast. But looking out of the cockpit, I could see the desert through occasional holes in the clouds and told myself I could pick up a landmark through the holes and land safely.

Our course was slightly east 30 miles, where I would drop in a westerly direction. On rocket burn-out I should be above Bakersfield, California, 90 miles west of the base, in position to turn and glide back to a landing. Cloud cover was now seven-tenths overcast and altitude 33,000 feet. With its heavy load, the B-50 would not go any higher. Captain Fulton nosed over to pick up speed for the drop and his dive carried him 2,800 feet toward the ground. At 7:45 A.M. he tripped the lever that released the bomb shackles in the big bomber and the X-2 fell free in the morning light.

My gloved fingers depressed the locking button on the throttle as I fell and locked it in full power position. With a force that slammed me back against the cockpit wall, both rocket chambers roared into life and the fiery energy thrust the falling airplane forward. Shaking my head to clear it from the shock of the sudden acceleration, I pulled the stick slowly back toward my pounding heart and began the familiar climb upward.

The X-2 leaped forward convulsively, eating air, and I knew at once that I could not hold it down. Today it hungered for the whole sky. This appetite for speed was ravenous and would not be denied. Again I attempted to keep a predetermined climb schedule, and again the airplane was running away from me. Fighting the controls, struggling to hold a steady flight path, at 50,000 feet I was already supersonic. Very carefully now, afraid of overcontrolling again, slowly I began the familiar push-over toward level flight.

Automatically I discounted the time lag in my altimeter and Machmeter. Speed was such that my instruments could not keep up with the fantastic acceleration. Altitude was 50,000 feet indicated, 55,000 true altitude. Rounding out now, I would be straight and level at 60,000 feet indicated, true 65,000.

All the instruments were lagging. I held the control stick with both hands, still pushing forward. My senses were extremely acute and drawn to one point in time, luminous and aware and waiting for the unknown to happen. In my hands I held the reins of 100,000 horses I was driving.

Level—now. Ready—now. The airplane accelerated on up and I watched the Machmeter climb to a speed I knew had never before been flown by man. I observed some debris coming over the nose of the plane and hitting the windshield. Worry now, until I thought of paint blistering and coming back over the cockpit. This was the heat barrier. A moment's quick concern, then my mind dismissed it.

I had no time to think about it now, I was too busy flying. The airplane handled beautifully. Still in level flight, it continued to drift on upward, hurled skyward by the incredible momentum of its climb. Speed was over 1,900 miles an hour. I felt like an explorer, like Columbus and Magellan. I was both awed and proud.

Except for the hiss of air over the cockpit and the faroff crackle of static over my radio headset, I heard nothing. Alone in a silent world, I was acutely conscious of absolute stillness and calmness, a solitary world above the earth and everything human. An occasional clicking whispered in my ears as the electrical instruments fed their invisible energy through the headset. Otherwise there was perfect silence and I had a suspended feeling of being alone in time and space and away from all things living.

Aided by the modified fuel probes, the rocket engine burned four seconds longer than ever before, then sucked the tanks bone-dry of fuel and burned out. As the X-2 drank itself empty, the thirsty rocket swallowed the last gallon of alcohol and shut down.

I pulsed the ailerons to the left, pulsed them to the right, then did a stabilizer pulse to the positive position. I could detect very little yaw tendency, but I noted a definite decay in lateral stability. When I released aileron pressure and returned the controls to neutral, the airplane continued rolling in the direction of the control movement, and I had to apply opposite control to stop the roll from continuing.

By pulsing the controls, I mean maneuvering, a movement of the stick. To pulse the ailerons I moved it sideways laterally and to pulse the stabilizer I moved it fore and aft directionally. If I pulsed the ailerons too far I knew from the GEDA machine that the X-2 might not stop rolling.

For this reason I pulsed the stick very gently, just an inch or two sideways, then returned it immediately to neutral to observe the reaction of the airplane. I pulsed it to the left again, then to the right. Then an inch or two in the rearward position on the stabilizer pulse. I noted that the airplane was still controllable and I felt it could be flown safely at these speeds or a little faster. However, control was marginal, and if the pilot overcontrolled or maneuvered the airplane too violently, anything could happen.

When I finally broke radio silence I said one word, "Bingo!" Unless I reported in code, which I forgot to do in my excitement, that was all I could say in the open. But to the listeners many miles below me, it said what they were waiting to hear. This was it—this time we had done it! They knew then that I had approached the higher Mach numbers we hoped to reach.

Glancing quickly out of the cockpit at the toy landscape far below me, I tried to identify my position over the California desert. Although at extreme altitude, looking at the distant earth I thought I could make out the city of Bakersfield. I reported to my chase pilots and asked if they had me in sight, but they did not. Without the exhaust from my rocket engine, they no longer had the guide by which they tracked me, and I was too high and far away for them to see me now.

Giving them what I thought was my position over Bakersfield, I made a right turn back toward Edwards and began my letdown. Speed was still supersonic, and again I performed aileron and stabilizer pulses to test control and stability of the airplane, being extremely careful not to overcontrol. Although engine power was off, there had not been an appreciable lessening of my momentum, as deceleration in the rarified air was a slow decay. It was several minutes later and altitude was below 50,000 feet before the X-2 was subsonic again.

At 30,000 feet now, I did more maneuvers, approaching stall and then pulling up to test dive recovery, but my mind wasn't really on my work today. Instead my head was filled with thoughts of the speed I had just attained, faster than any man had ever flown, and my heart was filled with emotions of awe and pride. I felt that I had made a contribution to mankind, a small step forward in aeronautical science—perhaps another step toward the time when men will fly in space. This was a niche I had made for myself, and I was proud of it. It was a warm happy feeling, one that I did not want to have alone.

Although I could not disclose my true speed over the radio for security reasons, I left no doubt that my flight had been a successful one. Congratulatory messages filled my headset, and when my chase pilots picked me up I did a few victory rolls, even turning in to them playfully in my wonderful feeling of exuberance and achievement.

At 20,000 feet we entered the overcast, breaking clear again at 16,000, where below me to the east lay the familiar runways of the dry lake. Waiting down there—as they always had—to see me safely home again, were the wonderful people who made this flight possible. It made me feel good to know I had not let them down. And also waiting for me, still unseen but felt more keenly than ever, were Avis and home.

Making my last landing at Edwards Air Force Base, I came in low over the key point, chase planes with me and Major Childs talking me in. On the ground now, I touched down in a cloud of dust and skidded to a smooth stop, just fifteen minutes after drop from the B-50 a life ago. Jimmy Dunn and his mechanics came running up to take off the canopy and Jimmy Powell helped me out of the cockpit, grinning and shaking my hand, while the others crowded around to slap me on the back and ask a thousand questions.

Standing beside the X-2, I tried to answer them all at once. For the first time I was able to reveal the exact speed I attained on today's flight. Partly to celebrate it, but also because they had worked around the clock and needed a rest, Sil Sartore, the Bell manager at Edwards, declared a three-day holiday for all company employees. Then the airplane that had become so much a part of me was lifted on its handling dolly and towed to the hangar across the field. I climbed in the Bell jeep between Jimmy Powell and Bob Lapp, and with a final look at the X-2, returned to my office for the last time.

The first thing I did was telephone Avis and tell her the good news. Then I didn't know how to say it. "Honey, you are talking to the fastest man in the world," I said finally. When I told her we had made a successful flight, she was just as happy as I was.

Inspection of the X-2 revealed that the high-temperature paint on the leading edges had been scorched and blistered severely, as if someone had held a blowtorch against the airplane. We also were able to measure the high-speed heating by the temperature pickup gauges. From these different readings we knew what temperatures had developed at maximum speed, and they were not as high as had been anticipated.

Of course, I was at top speed only a short period of time, and when my engine quit the speed dropped off at once. It was just like running your finger through the flame of a match. You can run your finger through the flame fairly rapidly and not suffer any damage. But if you were to move your finger slowly or hold it in the flame, you would get burned.

We were not trying to go fast for the sake of speed alone or the glory of making a record. We were running stability tests and increasing the Mach number in successive stages to see the result—whether the stability curves would fall along the lines predicted by wind-tunnel studies.

We learned from our flights that stability of the airplane was slightly better than predicted. This stability was now no longer just a wind-tunnel prediction—a theory—but a fact. And we could give this information to aircraft manufacturers who were designing new planes to fly at these Mach numbers.

As a result of our experience, they know that an airplane of the X-2 design has attained specific speeds and altitudes and remained stable. They need not be concerned about the unknown any longer, because men in an airplane have reached these speeds and come back safely. This far, at least, the unknown is no more.

After reducing the records and studying them, we knew my flight path could have been better, as I never reached true level flight during maximum acceleration. I could have gone even faster, as I was still climbing. As a result of my experience, I felt that another pilot might be able to make his run in true level flight. If he could fly the X-2 under the same conditions and get the extra time out of his fuel tanks, he could increase my speed. However, I wrote in my report that so far as I was concerned, this concluded the high-speed part of the X-2 flight test program.

As I took off my pressure suit and hung it up, it was with the realization that I would not wear it again. But I was convinced in my own mind that the X-2 still had more speed left in it. By pushing over faster and getting the airplane in level flight sooner, it was my feeling that they could increase the speed.

I expressed this opinion to Colonel Hanes when I reported to his office to discuss the flight. As we had now gotten a good speed run out of the X-2, Captain Kincheloe would conduct the high-altitude program. But when this was completed and if time and money permitted, I thought that Captain Apt might renew the high-speed program with good results.

Colonel Hanes asked me if I would like to stay for another flight to get higher speeds, but I said no. If today's flight had not been successful I would have accepted. But as things stood, the flight worked out, and I did not feel justified in delaying my departure a second time. With an engine change required on the B-50, and the Bell people almost exhausted, it would be a good week before the X-2 could fly again, and I felt I should continue to my new station.

Colonel Hanes agreed with me. I told him good-by and left for the Bell hangar for postflight critique and pilot briefing. Back at my desk again, I made out my pilot's report, collected the few personal belongings still remaining, then left my office for the last time.

Cindy and Vicky were at school when I got home, but five-year-old Kendall was in the yard digging a slit trench. Avis ran out to the driveway as I jumped from the car and hugged and kissed me. Her eyes were shining with joy and relief, because she knew now we really were going.

Over the luncheon table I still talked about the flight that morning, and she tried to appear interested. But I knew her heart wasn't in it, and after a while I began talking about other things. Besides, the movers were coming tomorrow, and I had to help her do the packing.

13

The Race for Space

Avis felt that it was time to go, that I had done enough. She felt I had risked my neck with all the test flights I had made in the past, and that I had contributed enough to the progress of aviation. However, she had not complained. She knew this was my dream and had not forced me to go; she did not want me to leave against my wishes. I think she realized that I had to make the maximum effort possible toward a new record before moving on to a new assignment, and she did not force me to compromise my desires and ambitions.

Several years later, and after losing two lives and four airplanes, we know what caused the fires and explosions that destroyed three X-1 rocket ships and the first X-2. Wendell Moore, the Bell rocket engineer, solved the problem after the crash of the X-1A in 1955 during the NACA test program.

These explosions were caused by the impregnated leather gaskets used for sealing liquid oxygen joints such as tank inspection doors and vent valves. The impregnating material in the leather gaskets was sensitive to shock forces or pressures in the presence of liquid oxygen, and exploded if struck sharply or loaded suddenly. This touched off a chain reaction that caused an explosion in the liquid oxygen tanks, followed by fire and a water-alcohol explosion. As a result of Moore's discovery, the leather seals were replaced with a noncombustible material in the three remaining Bell rocket planes and no further damage has resulted.

His invaluable detective work, which has undoubtedly saved other lives and airplanes, quite possibly including my own, was typical of the great contribution to aeronautical research made by Bell Aircraft Corporation. Bell built new pioneering research planes with full awareness that production contracts would not be forthcoming. This of course meant that these planes would never be profitable because they would not be built in quantity. In fact, many manufacturers have refused even to consider building research planes because there is no profit in it. Yet Larry Bell and his associates unselfishly continued to build and fly these aircraft which have done so much to advance aviation. Without them we would still be flying at Mach 2 or less.

Both airplanes were important and accomplished something new. Each was designed for a specific job and achieved its mission. The X-1 was a straight-wing airplane and gave us needed data on a straight-wing design in supersonic flight. It could not have accomplished the same results as the X-2, however, even if it had the same performance. The X-2 gave us data on a sweptwing airplane at high speeds. It also gave us an opportunity to test this design at higher speeds because it had the capability of going faster.

The X-2 was flown four times after I left Edwards. Captain Iven Kincheloe made three more flights and established a new altitude record of 126,200 feet. In September Captain Milburn Apt made his first flight in the X-2 and was able to exceed my speed. However, the airplane went out of control and crashed, killing the pilot.

Many people have asked me why I did this work. What was the challenge to me? Why did I want to be the fastest man alive?

Basically I believe there are two principal answers to these questions—I enjoyed the work, and I desired to excel. I like to fly more than anything in the world, and this means military flying. I would rather be in the Air Force, contributing to the good of the nation, than be a millionaire—although I am not averse to money. Each man's fulfillment is pleasure in his work, and I have always enjoyed mine. Our goal should be contentment and satisfaction in the work we do, and if you have the right job, the rest is easy.

As for the other part of it, I am an average man with ambition to succeed, who worked hard to do so. This ambition may go back to man's basic nature. It is my opinion that every human being has an urge to better his position in the world. I believe that man's natural instinct is to better himself, and by so doing he will better all mankind.

It was my purpose to create something, to make a contribution. One man may want to be an outstanding painter; another may wish to amass great wealth; as for me, the contribution I could make to aviation progress was the measurement of my personal progress and creative efforts toward bettering my own position in life. My work was a challenge to fly better and do something no pilot had ever done before.

My reward is pride in my own ability as a pilot, the feeling of contributing to man's progress and perhaps the betterment of all men. Not just to the Air Force or my own country, but to the over-all effort of the world toward something better—to the progress of humanity, of all mankind.

It was a reward to know that I had placed myself in a small niche that no one had ever reached before—that I had done something new. I felt that in the future I could be proud of what I had done—and my children and grandchildren would remember my contribution and be proud of my accomplishments. I feel that I have approached upon the shores of space. I have walked through the sand on the beach, looking out over the turbulent and stormy seas on which we will soon embark.

I have been asked many times what it takes to be a test pilot. I think the most important requirement is the desire to be one. This is 99 per cent of the answer. After that, of course, you need the ability. I have known many people who wanted to be test pilots but did not possess the qualifications. Desire and ability are most important. After that experience, education, and training are secondary.

The perfect test pilot would be a man who is twenty-one years old, has 5,000 hours of jet time in a hundred different airplanes, and also has a master's or doctor's degree in aeronautical engineering. Realizing that this is impossible, you have to sit in judgment and take the next best.

Age to me has a lot to do with test flying. I always preferred that no one be assigned to me at Edwards who was not thirty years or younger—preferably younger. For a fighter test pilot I would rather have a young pilot with only two years of college and 1,500 hours of flying than a man many years older with an engineering degree and twice the experience. For bombers and cargo planes, age is not as important.

At age thirty I have found that most pilots start down, including myself; their reaction time, their outlook, and their mental processes start declining. They don't necessarily lose their enthusiasm and ability for flight testing, but they definitely gain more desire to continue living.

In fighter and experimental flight testing, the best pilots are the younger men. They have the fearlessness and readiness to take chances that you need in flight testing. I know that in the early years I myself was much more willing to take risks than on the day I made my last flight in the X-2. As a pilot becomes older and more mature, with a family and other responsibilities, he thinks twice about risking his life. It becomes more important to him. As he grows older, he wants to live longer, realizing that time is passing and perhaps half of his life is behind him. For this reason it is natural for him to want to live to enjoy the remaining years. This is just a natural maturity I believe everyone experiences.

Of course there are exceptions. There are pilots who never slow down. There are individuals such as General Boyd, who is still flying all types of research planes and new supersonic jet fighters in his early fifties, while at the same time there are people in their twenties who do not desire this hazardous work and lack the mental attitude required to accomplish it successfuly. It is all a matter of the individual.

In my case, the experience of ten years in test flying made it much easier for me to accomplish what I did. In other words, it would be difficult if not impossible to take a pilot thirty-five years old with little or no jet time and testing experience and expect him to be in the mental condition to test rocket planes. He would probably be completely out of his element and unable to perform the mission.

But if you could take a man with my background and experience in test flying and make him ten years younger than I was—then you might be able to accomplish even more. There would be a little less feeling of apprehension on the part of the pilot, and he in turn would perhaps subject himself to a little more risk.

We will always need pilots to fly research planes and

ilitary and commercial aircraft and to monitor missiles. We
ill also need men to test these airplanes and space ships
efore they can be put into service. For this reason flight
sting will always be a part of aviation. It cannot be done
way with.

We are constantly increasing the performance capabilities
f new planes, and as speed increases, many "bugs" will
ave to be worked out before the planes can be used for
ilitary or commercial purposes. It will fall to test pilots to
o this hazardous but necessary work—and primarily to the
ilitary test pilot. He will be selected because he has more
xperience than civilian pilots in different types of aircraft
nd more opportunities to fly them.

However, as aircraft performance continues to increase, I
ink we must radically change our concepts of the nature and
esponsibilities of flight testing. In the future the test pilot
ill have to specialize. His is a highly trained, technical
rofession, requiring unusual skills and attitudes, with pre-
ium on knowledge and experience.

For this reason the future test pilot must be carefully
elected for the job and must stay in the same job for a longer
me. In military testing, I believe a pilot should be assigned
arly in his career, after taking a college degree in aero-
autical engineering and spending several years in a tactical
rganization to get flight experience. Then he should remain
 test pilot as long as he is physically and mentally capable of
oing the job. The present system of constant change to new
ssignments no longer is adequate. With aircraft speeds con-
antly increasing, test flying will become more and more
ifficult. We should retain the test pilot in the same job as
ong as he remains qualified, to take advantage of the skill
nd experience he gains over the years.

His role, although dangerous, will be a highly necessary
ne. He will be expected to go to speeds and altitudes never
efore reached by man. He will also be expected to report on
hat is occurring at these speeds and altitudes. Moreover, he
ill be expected to make recommendations for the modifica-
on and design of high-speed planes to combat problems that
ill be encountered at still greater speeds and heights.

As he flies higher, of course, he will subject himself to
ther hazards—the extreme cold and absolute zero temper-

atures encountered when traveling into space. At the same time he will be subjected to extremely high temperature resulting from air friction at high speeds in the earth's at mosphere, and radiation from the sun at extreme heights. For these reasons, he will be forced to test many new kinds of clothing and equipment developed to protect human being against these hazards. And if he flies at great heights for any length of time he must be protected against severe burns.

He will also encounter entirely new problems of control. How do we control an airplane at these higher speeds and altitudes? How do we change its direction of flight, in air so thin that ordinary control surfaces have absolutely no effect on its flight path? And once we get into space and the airplane is coasting on its own momentum, floating in space with nothing to stop it, how do we turn it around and head back toward earth again? These are some of the problems ahead of us in aviation. I am sure it is obvious to the reader that we are going to need experienced test pilots who can specialize in these problems if we hope to solve them.

After the new airplanes have been tested and put into service, we are also going to need pilots to fly them. Of course, as speeds increase and automatic flight equipment is developed further, it is obvious that the role of the pilot will change. He will become more like a monitor of a missile. Aside from take-off and landing, he will play a lesser part in actually manipulating and maneuvering the airplane. It will fly a predetermined flight path that will be carried out almost entirely by the use of automatic pilots. But if something goes wrong, on earth or in space, we will need a human being to monitor the emergency. He will attempt to correct the problem, and if unable to do so, will take action to save the passengers and crew.

To me the Air Force has a considerable amount to offer a young man looking for a lifetime career. Although it is unlikely that he will become wealthy in the service, he will achieve satisfaction and fulfillment in life, knowing that he has done a good job and served his country.

He will deal with people and with new developments in aviation. No matter what his assignment, he will live a part of flying. Even if he is a Post Exchange officer, for example, he will serve the people who fly and maintain airplanes. And of course he won't be a PX officer forever. In the meantime he is playing a necessary part in the advancement of aviation.

The young man in his teens today who later becomes an Air Force pilot will grow up to participate in space flight. And from that beginning he may be instrumental in organizing airlines for trips to other planets. He can look out into space and know it is an unlimited field for growth. All a young man needs to do is to attach himself to the Air Force or aircraft industry, to be part of the tremendous growth that is coming in aviation.

It goes without saying that we will also have airplanes in the future, both military and commercial. However, the guided missile will take over many duties of the fighter plane. The recent decision of the British government to concentrate on missiles and bombers and discontinue the production of fighter types is a trend that all countries eventually will follow. We will continue to need defensive fighters for a long time, but the missile will take over the role of the fighter-bomber. Day fighters will be the first to go. Their passing will cause many tears to flow, as all true fighter pilots desire to fly them. However, the all-weather fighter will shortly take over the role played by the day fighter.

The airplane will continue to look very much like the present supersonic jet fighters and bombers. Of course its performance will be increased many times. Using rocket engines or a combination of rockets and jet engines, we will be able to span the oceans in two or three hours. The rocket engine will be the principal type of power plant for all long-range flights. This will include flights between continents on the earth as well as flight into space.

The sweptwing design is a thing of the past for new rocket planes. It was adopted to delay the effects of compressibility in subsonic flight, and for this purpose it proved highly useful. But with the speed provided by the rocket engine the rocket plane accelerates so rapidly that compressibility is less a problem. Swept wings will of course continue to have practical application in jet transport aircraft that fly under or slightly above the speed of sound.

The rocket engine is just now coming into its own. Much research is being done but it should be increased. While rocket engine development at present is limited to missiles and other military applications, we should also be designing engines, air frames, control systems, and protective devices for air crews to take us into space itself.

In the meantime, the traveling public can expect to fly in rocket planes on long flights to earthly destinations. Because of its great speed, the rocket engine is not practical for commercial flights over shorter distances. The jet engine will continue to be used for medium and long-range flights in a secondary role. The turboprop engine will also be used on medium and short routes, together with the reciprocating-type piston engine.

The lack of power plants to take the air frames to higher speeds and altitudes is one of the major barriers to faster flight at the present time. Another barrier is the lack of adequate control systems to maneuver the airplane at higher speeds and altitudes. A third barrier is man himself. How are we going to protect our pilots and crews? This is of prime importance. The test pilot often takes undue risks to get essential data on new aircraft. But these risks are not acceptable for normal operations, either military or commercial. Until we are able to provide maximum flight safety for the people on board, we will have to sacrifice speed and altitude.

There has been considerable discussion of a so-called heat barrier. I feel there is no such thing as a heat barrier or thermal thicket. Heat is only a restriction on faster flight. At present it is a problem at lower altitudes with aircraft metals now available. But as we develop new metals and engines capable of sustaining flight at higher altitudes, surface heating will no longer be a restriction. Above 60,000 feet, drag ceases for all practical purposes; and at 120 miles—about 600,000 feet—above the earth, there is no longer air resistance of any sort.

Military aircraft have gone through a series of speed restrictions since the advent of the jet engine. The early jets, the straight-wing F-80 and F-84, were restricted by compressibility. If they went too fast shock waves occurred that caused the ailerons and tail surfaces to flutter. The first sweptwing airplane in America, the F-86, was restricted by high Q pressures, caused by dense air below 10,000 feet.

Some of the new Century series fighters are restricted by stability. They are designed to fly to certain speeds, but a few have the power to go faster. When they reach their design limit speed they become unstable and could go out of control. For this reason, they are restricted.

At this writing, the F-104 jet fighter is the only airplane in this country that is restricted by heat. And this heat restriction is on the engine, not the air frame. Published reports have stated that the 104 can fly at Mach 2, which is twice the speed of sound, or more than 1,500 miles an hour at sea level. If the present engine can be improved or a new engine can be developed to withstand higher temperatures without suffering damage, then the airplane may be permitted to go faster. It has the capability but is restricted by the critical engine temperature.

The principal barrier to faster flight is the human barrier —the ability of the human being to react fast enough to control the airplane. The basic problem is the speed of human reactions. Flying at very high speeds at Mach 3 and above, the man-airplane is an integral unit. What are its limits? The pilot must close the control loop with human nerves and muscles. Is he sensitive and fast enough to do so? In the event of trouble, can he control the behavior of the airplane and retain command of the situation? From my own experience in the X-2, we know that man can retain control at speeds near Mach 3, or 1,900 miles an hour. We also know that another pilot lost control in the same airplane going a little faster. As of now the limiting factor appears to be the ability of the pilot to control the airplane in high-speed maneuvers and high G forces.

Despite these limitations, today airpower is mankind's major weapon because it can reach any point on earth with the irresistible force of nuclear bombs. The airplane is still the best vehicle we have for delivering these awesome explosives. At such time as long-range guided missiles have been perfected to do the same job, then the piloted bomber will play a secondary role. But air weapons as such will continue to be supreme.

Although airpower is supreme, however, it is not absolute. By this I mean it does not eliminate the need for land and sea forces. All three are necessary for a proper balance of military power. We need the ships and naval convoys to deliver troops and supplies to overseas bases, and we need ground forces to clean up pockets of enemy resistance and occupy enemy territory. For these reasons we will continue to need both an Army and a Navy.

I also believe they should continue to function as three, or at a minimum, two separate services. It is theoretically possible that we could reorganize our armed forces into offensive and defensive branches and still give the country the protection that is needed. In such an organization, for example, the Air Defense Command, the Army's missile units, and the Navy's picket ships and off-shore patrol planes would all be part of a single defense command, while the Strategic Air Command, the navy's carriers and offensive surface vessels and the Army's air-borne and armored units would be combined in one offensive striking force.

The other alternative is one armed force with land, sea, and air units. This would be unification on a high level. You would have a single Chief of Staff and everybody wearing the same uniform, but it would still come down more or less to what you have today—a Defense Department with land, sea, and air forces. I don't think it would gain much. I don't agree with the single Chief of Staff concept. If the job went to a man who was prejudiced in favor of a particular service, and ignorant or indifferent to the needs and functions of the other services, he could ruin the military establishment and possibly cost us another war in the future. To me this is the most important argument against complete unification of the armed forces.

Several times during my career, flying at high altitudes above the earth, I saw objects in the sky that looked like flying saucers—objects from another planet. I immediately pursued them at maximum speed in an effort to intercept and identify them and report my findings.

On every occasion but one, however, they turned out to be familiar objects—other aircraft flying at very high altitudes, weather balloons drifting through the stratosphere, or classified objects of earthly origin. There was just one time when I was unable to identify an unknown aerial object, and I was on the ground and unable to give chase.

From what I know, I do not believe that flying saucers exist. I believe there is life on other planets, possibly quite advanced beyond our own, and it is possible that we have been under observation for many years by people from other worlds. But this belief is an opinion and is not based on any evidence. So if other beings are watching us, I feel sure they are still unknown to us. However, I am open-minded on the subject, and at such time as we make contact with visitors from other planets, I will not be surprised to learn that they have been using the mysterious objects we call flying saucers.

I expect to see space travel in my lifetime. A high official from the Defense Department was quoted recently as saying we can realize space travel within ten years *if there is a reason to go there*. I wonder where we would be now if Columbus or the Wright brothers had felt this way? With my background and experience in flight testing and my interest in space flight, it has always been my dream to be the first man to land on the moon. If at such time I can serve my country better by doing so, it is my desire that I be returned to participate in the development of a manned satellite or rocket airplane to be flown into outer space.

Although we should have an unmanned satellite in space within a few months, we are lagging behind in the exploration of space. We should have studies, tests, and programs under way now to build a satellite that will carry human beings.

I feel very strongly about this because of my conviction that the first man in space will control the earth. He need not come from a large or powerful nation. Even a small and comparatively weak nation can achieve world domination with a manned spaceship armed with nuclear guided missiles. Given these two essentials, such a nation could then launch a nuclear attack against the earth with no possibility of retaliation and enforce unconditional surrender.

When this happens, it will change warfare as we know it. Today the big bomber armed with nuclear weapons is the major deterrent to aggression; what will it be tomorrow? When the first manned spaceship is a reality, armed with an ISBM—Inter-Satellite Ballistic Missile—neither bombers nor missiles based on the earth will be able to prevent war by threat of retaliation.

This is the beginning of the race for space. For man must look beyond his little earth in war and peace. In the not-distant future, he must control space to protect himself from aggression. And beyond that lies the need for new worlds to sustain life. With the earth's population continually increasing, it will some day reach the limit of its capacity to support him.

When that time comes, man must turn to other worlds which lie waiting for him beyond the sky. It is to reach these worlds that we must go on building new wings for flight tomorrow.

The End

A Note About
The Bantam Air &
Space Series

This is the era of flight—the century which has seen man soar, not only into the skies of Earth but beyond the gravity of his home planet and out into the blank void of space. An incredible accomplishment achieved in an incredibly short time.

How did it happen?

The AIR & SPACE series is dedicated to the men and women who brought this fantastic accomplishment about, often at the cost of their lives—a library of books which will tell the grand story of man's indomitable determination to seek the new, to explore the farthest frontier.

The driving theme of the series is the skill of *piloting*, for without this, not even the first step would have been possible. Like the Wright Brothers and those who, for some 35 years, followed in their erratic flight path, the early flyers had to be designer, engineer and inventor. Of necessity, they were the pilots of the crazy machines they dreamt up and strung together.

Even when the technology became slightly more sophisticated, and piloting became a separate skill, the quality of a flyer's ability remained rooted in a sound working knowledge of his machine. World War I, with its spurt of development in aircraft, made little change in the role of the flyer who remained, basically, pilot-navigator-engineer.

Various individuals, like Charles Lindbergh, risked their lives and made high drama of the new dimension they were carving in the air. But still, until 1939, flying was a romantic, devil-may-care wonder, confined to a relative handful of hardy individuals. Commercial flight on a large scale was a mere gleam in the eye of men like Howard Hughes.

It took a second major conflict, World War II, from 1939 to 1945, to provoke the imperative that required new concepts from the designers—and created the arena where hundreds of young men and women would learn the expertise demanded by high-speed, high-tech aircraft.

From the start of flight, death has taken its toll. Flying has always been a high-risk adventure. Never, since men first launched themselves into the air, has the new element given up its sacrifice of stolen lives, just as men have never given up the driving urge to go farther, higher, faster. Despite only a fifty-fifty chance of any mission succeeding, *still* the dream draws many more men and women to spaceflight than any program can accommodate. And still, in 1969, when Mike Collins, Buzz Aldrin and Neil Armstrong first took man to the Moon, the skill of piloting, sheer flying ability, was what actually landed the "Eagle" on the Moon's surface. And still, despite technological sophistication undreamed of 30 or 40 years earlier, despite demands on any flyer for levels of performance and competence and the new understanding of computer science not necessary in early aircraft, it is piloting, *human* control of the aircraft—sometimes, indeed, inspired control—that remains the major factor in getting there and back safely.

From this rugged breed of individualists come the bush pilots of today, men who even now fly their little planes above the vast, icy expanse of the Arctic, landing in small open stretches, on wheels, skis, or pontoons, carrying with them all the spare parts they need to repair their own craft. The first of the AIR & SPACE series is about one such pilot—THE LAST OF THE BUSH PILOTS, by Harmon Helmericks.

The horrors of World War II bred and trained literally hundreds of pilots. Here the expertise of piloting in life and death situations began to teach the designers. FORK-TAILED DEVIL: THE P38, by Martin Caidin, was a fighter plane whose deficiencies cost lives until its pilots used their combat experience to correct its faults. On the other hand, there was the unbelievable strength of the War's greatest bomber, the Flying Fort. Pilots called it the airplane you could trust. It too, saw improvement both in design and effectiveness that was a direct result of battle, and the Fort brought its bomber crews home when the problem lay not so much in flying the monster as in landing an aircraft that was half shot away. . . . FLYING FORTS: THE B-17 IN WORLD WAR II by Martin Caidin, tells the magnificent, edge-of-the-seat story of this fantastic aircraft.

The War also saw the start of a new kind of flying machine—one without propellers—for jet propulsion was born at this time. And very secretly, right after the close of hostilities, Chuck Yeager was busy testing the X-1 and breaking the sound barrier. This was just the beginning. Even the early test pilots of the U.S. Air Force carried the speed of piloted jet aircraft to 1,900 miles an hour—nearly three times the speed of sound. Frank Everest flew his X-2 at these incredible speeds, and as high as 60-odd miles. John Guenther, noted aviation writer, tells the story of Frank Everest in THE FASTEST MAN ALIVE.

After America first landed men on the Moon, the Russian space program pushed ahead with plans for eventually creating a permanent space station where men could live. And in 1982 they sent up two men—Valentin Lebedev and Anatoly Berezovoy—to live on Solyut-7 for seven months. This extraordinary feat has been recorded in the diaries of pilot Lebedev, DIARY OF A COSMONAUT: 211 DAYS IN SPACE by Valentin Lebedev.

The Bantam AIR & SPACE series will include several titles by or about flyers from all over the world—and about the planes they flew, including World War II, the postwar era of barnstorming and into the jet age, plus the personal histories of many of the world's greatest pilots. Man is still the most important element in flying.

A NOTE ABOUT
THE AUTHOR

John Guenther

An author and former journalist, John Guenther has written extensively on aviation from his long experience as an Air Force officer in World War II and postwar aircraft executive. He has drawn on this intimate knowledge of military and commercial aviation in writing about the early days of flying in this country and the legendary pilots who tested our first jet and rocket planes. Their pioneering exploits helped pave the way to space flight, and Guenther coined the phrase, "the race for space", in telling their life stories. As a journalist, he wrote for Scripps-Howard newspapers, the United Press and *Newsweek* magazine, and following military service, has published some dozen books of biography, fiction, poetry and drama here and abroad. A native of Ann Arbor, Michigan, he attended the University of Illinois and Harvard, and makes his home in New York City.

Here is a preview of the next volume in the Air and Space Series, *DIARY OF A COSMONAUT: 211 Days in Space* by Valentin Lebedev.

From the beginning of our exploration of the frontiers of our domain, our sights have always been set on the horizon. From the land we looked to the sea, from the sea to the skies, and from the skies to the stars. It has been a journey that has, with each achievement, grown rather than diminished, with no end in sight.

With the launching of the orbiting Soviet artificial space satellite *Sputnik 1* on October 4, 1957, the inhabitants of Earth entered the space age. We colonized foreign lands, but could we colonize foreign realms? The race had begun to become more than visitors, to become true residents in the Great Unknown.

Diary of a Cosmonaut is the personal chronicle of Russian cosmonaut Valentin Lebedev, who, with his comrade, Anatoly Berezovoy, spent 211 days in outer space aboard the space station *Salyut-7* from May to December of 1982. Following is an excerpt from flight engineer Lebedev's personal journal. . . .

MAY 11

The days have been sunny and warm and the nights cool. Since I sleep with the window open, I was cold last night and didn't sleep well.

Today is an important day—the State Commission gives its final approval to the flight crew. In its usual ceremonial way, the Commission announced its decision to assign Tolia and me as the main crew on the *Salyut*-7 station. Shatalov announced the decision, then everyone congratulated us. In our acceptance speech we spoke of the great honor that it was for us to begin work on the *Salyut*-7 station and to pave the way for future crews. We also said that we realized the flight would be difficult but interesting. We will do everything possible to honorably fulfill the task that our country has given us. After the State Commission meeting we had a press conference. An anticlimax to the previous meeting. Dull and boring.

Tonight I called Cosmonaut Yeliseyev. He was happy to hear from me and asked if there was anything that he could do for me. I told him that I had only one thing to ask: I wanted him to help me establish from the very beginning good friendly relations with the FCC (Flight Control Center) and, in case something should go wrong, to try to understand and help us.

I took a little walk before going to sleep and during the walk I thought about all I went through to get to my second spaceflight. I've come a long way through the maze of human relationships, troubles, training, and retraining on new equipment; through failures and pitfalls; and now I have reached the summit. I still feel scared. Not because of the position I've reached, not because of the danger that faces everyone in this profession, not because of the length of the flight or the vast amount of work. I'm scared of myself. Can I live and work with my crewmate in such a confined space for so long? Will I fail? It seemed that the main problems were behind me; now I see they're still ahead. Well, we aren't the first. Many people have already gone this way.

When I talked to Lusia, I felt irritated, and this came across. She asked me a lot about how I'm doing but didn't talk much about home. My darling, she'll understand me.

I asked our doctor, Eugeniy Kobzev, "What do you think? Will we handle it?"

"I don't know," he replied.

Deep inside of me I know that we can handle it. I am just looking for some reassurance.

Yura Masiukov, our coach, told me, "Sure you'll handle it, but somewhere in the middle of the flight you can expect a breakdown. Later, though, everything will get back to normal."

MAY 12

I didn't sleep well at all—yesterday's thoughts and emotions wouldn't go away. The weather was good. A light haze.

For exercise I ran, but Tolia stayed in his room.

In the morning Eugeniy Kobzev and I went to ask

him how he was doing. His upper lip was swollen; luckily his mustache camouflaged the swelling.

I told him, "Don't worry, Tolia, we'll fly. I'll carry you to the rocket if I have to."

He smiled. I understand him. It's especially hard for him because he doesn't know what lies ahead. I felt exactly the same way before my first spaceflight.

After lunch we watched a movie, *White Sun of the Desert*—that's our tradition. It is an interesting, optimistic, and human movie. Even the words from its song suit us: "Your Kindness, Lady Luck! To one you're a gentle mistress; to another you're cruel. . . ." Every one of us has at least once experienced that uncanny cruelty. I did, several years ago when I sprained my ankle on the trampoline just before launch day and didn't fly. But now I strongly believe in our luck, Tolia's and mine.

After the movie we went for a walk on the riverbank. We enjoyed a beautiful view. The river curved to the right. On the left over the flat steppe, a blue sky and a setting sun. On the other side of the river there was a lonely *yurt* (a nomad tent, like a tepee or wigwam made from animal skin or sheep felt—*Ed.*) of a Kazakh, a hermit who doesn't want to give up his free life in nature even though he's close to the city.

Tolia, Eugeniy, and I had a man-to-man conversation. We promised always to use our common sense and to try to stay friends. We came back to the hotel and had a sauna. After that a one-liter enema ended our preparation for flight. Then we had a massage. Now Tolia is tuning a radio in his room, and I'm finishing the last diary entries I'll make on Earth.

Leonov came and said, "Tomorrow you can sleep as long as you want. Ahead of you lie two difficult days of flight on the spaceship before docking."

MAY 13
Launch Day

Nine years of hard work behind me. Hooray! I am on top of the world. I feel great! The weather is beautiful.

Doctor Kobzev woke us up at ten minutes before nine, local time. The other doctors came and very smoothly performed a quick ten-minute checkup; everything was normal. My pulse was 66, blood pressure 100/75, and temperature 36.2°C.

Tolia stuck his head in the door and asked, "How is everything?"

"Fine. And how about you?"

"I'm fine too."

Great! Tolia had recovered from his cold sore.

I am not worrying at all, but I feel the importance of this day. My spirits were still high when I came back. I sunbathed by the pool. After the morning medical checkup all the obstacles were left behind. The road to space is open—here we go! I feel an incredible sense of calm, which I don't understand.

Before we left for the launch, our backup men (the guys working on the French program and Leonov) came to our room. Everybody sat down. I asked our doctor to bring bread, salt, and water to keep our family tradition. We slapped our knees and, with the words "into the saddle," we stood up, wrote our names on the hotel door, and went to the bus.

A Letter Home Before Launch

My dear family,

I am going on my mission. Nine years of worry and work are left behind. I am happy and calm; I feel great.

I'm sure that I can manage this, the greatest mission of my life. You are always with me; thank you for being so wonderful. You are my family. I kiss all of you. I kiss you, Mom. And Mom, give a kiss to my sisters, Valera, and Yulia for me, and say hello to all my friends and colleagues.

Your Valentin,
May 13, 1982

The Oath I Took Before the Flight

I will always remember:

1. In any difficult situation that might occur on board, I must follow my head, not my heart.
2. I won't speak or act hastily.
3. If Tolia is in the wrong, I will find it in myself to hold out my hand to him; if I'm in the wrong, I will be strong enough to admit it.
4. I will remember that my crewmate also deserves respect because of his hard work. He has a good family, friends, and people who believe in him.
5. In any circumstance I will keep my self-control; I will not speak or act harshly.
6. The success of the mission depends on us, and only by the work we both do will they judge me as a cosmonaut and as a man.
7. I believe that I am a strong-willed, intelligent person and can properly complete this mission—I've come a long way to get here.

After putting on our spacesuits we talked with the State Commission. One of its members asked me, "Where is your old spacesuit?"

I didn't hear him very well through my helmet. I answered, "I've already forgotten where it is."

"You're kidding," he said with a smile.

After that we got on the bus waiting near the MIK gate. We went out onto the concrete, as we did on my first flight. Only back then it was freezing and a bus was inside the MIK, but now we are going through the empty building. We passed through the gate and saw many people standing there. We approached the chairman of the State Commission. There we stood at attention on the concrete—spacecraft commander and on-board engineer. Tolia gave a report. Without shaking hands or hugging we immediately got onto the bus. The epidemiological service is very strict, and you can't do it any other way, not even for the chairman of the State Commission—we would be in space half a year.

We rode the bus to the launch site. Leonov and the

backup cosmonauts were with us. I got off the bus first, and a fuel truck passed right next to me.

My friends yelled to me, "Valentin, don't go any farther, return to the bus."

I thought about returning but remembered the superstition and went ahead. (He remembered a superstition that it's bad luck to return after you've started a long journey.—*Ed.*)

We reached the rocket elevator. The weather was beautiful. Everybody wished us off with *Ni pukha, ni pera* ("May nothing be left of you, neither down nor feather").

"Go to hell," we replied. (This whole exchange is like telling an actor to "break a leg." Russians believe if somebody wishes you good luck, you have to send him to hell, otherwise you will have bad luck.—*Ed.*)

We got in the elevator and went up. As we passed the stair landings, we saw some workers on duty and some rocket specialists waving to us. When the elevator stopped, the main designer of the spacecraft was already waiting for us. We went through a tunnel to the hatch door of the living compartment. I entered the descent module immediately, and Tolia followed. The hatch slowly closed.

Minus two hours was announced, but we weren't nervous. The spacecraft shook like a racing horse under a rider. I felt vibration through my back and my elbows on the armchair. Five minutes before launch they turned on the music. I felt peaceful without any emotions.

Launch was set from 13:06:47 to 13:06:53 and now, just three minutes before launch, I am writing in my diary. Vitalik and his classmates went camping. I am thinking about my family, and I know they are thinking about me.

Ignition. From somewhere below I hear the roaring wave of thundering thrust coming from blasting rocket engines. The rocket begins to sway to the left and to the right as if it were losing balance. Then we rise above the launchpad. We feel the loss of support. There was a two- to three-second delay, and then, all at once, the rocket takes off like it was suddenly unchained, and we yell, "Go-o-o-!"

The separation of the first stage went smoothly; we heard only a slight knock. Gravity was in excess of 2 G. Separations of the remaining stages were pretty rough, though, especially the third stage.

Little Note from Kovalenok

Valentin, I wish you a great journey. Good luck. Good luck. Good luck. Remember, many of us will be with you, but on board there will be only the two of you. Take care of each other. Good luck, see you later.

Kovalenok
May 10, 1982

MAY 14

I woke up at 2 a.m. I know that during the eleventh orbit at 3:30 a.m. we'll go on the radio and FCC will tell us whether or not we should perform another maneuver.

Tolia was sleeping in the living compartment. I went to see how he was doing but he wasn't there. There were only our space suits hanging up to dry. I was puzzled. It was dark. I touched a space suit on the couch and found Tolia inside. I laughed—Tolia had crept inside the space suit because he was cold. Earlier I had tried to sleep in the descent module, first above the chair, then strapped into it. Then I took the straps off so I wouldn't feel how hard the chair was. Sometimes I stood spread-eagled against two walls. I didn't want to wake Tolia up, so I came back to the descent module and began to write in my diary.

The first thing that surprised me was that I didn't feel the uniqueness of everything around me. I don't even enjoy looking at the Earth, as if I go to space every month.

Every free moment Tolia looks out a window and is fascinated by everything, "Valia, look at this!"

I answer, "It's all right, we'll get enough of this in the next six months. The most important thing now is docking."

I can see that weightlessness has forced the blood into Tolia's head. His head is swollen, his hair sticks up, and his mustache is a mess. But we're healthy and happy. The most important thing today is docking, after that we will have a place to live and work. I have a good appetite here. I saw Tolia hanging in the living compartment, snoozing, his eyes closed and his shoulders lifted up like Jesus crucified.

"Tolia, eat something," I told him.

"No, I don't want to," he said and floated into the descent module to sleep until the maneuver should start.

So I hung our space suits up to dry and exercised with the inflated humanoid shapes around me. It seemed as if all three of us were working.

A communication period: Ground Control told us there would be an additional maneuver during the twelfth orbit, which means we don't get to sleep. Later we'll dock, the most important thing. At least we feel good.

We performed the maneuver by ourselves by following the computations from the FCC because the engine had to be turned on beyond the visual zone, the zone of the FCC control. This fact causes great concern to the people at the FCC, and we understand that.

We performed the maneuver very well. We approached the station. The orbit was 194 km × 240 km. Then, after a third thrust from the impulse engine, we began to fly at an altitude I'd never been before.

I looked through a porthole; we were flying over the ocean. There was a 1,000-km-long veil of translucent clouds like a spider's web stretched over the cumulus clouds above the ocean.

The first shift in the Flight Control Center went off duty. We enjoyed working with them very much; I have to find out who they were.

We used the data from the on-board computer in our approach to the station. The distance from the station was 457 km. The *Mera* radiotechnical system, a long-range scanner, switched on at a distance of 250 km.

Communication period. We reported that we had completed the two-impulse maneuver.

Mera hadn't locked on and we were leaving the zone. After testing *Mera* once more we immediately locked on; the calculations and *Mera's* data matched perfectly. The distance was 27 km, the speed was 45 m/sec. *Igla*, the short-range navigation system, turned on, locking onto the station. After this, our work was easy. We saw the station in the screen. It was 6 km away, a shiny dot, like a star with antennae whiskers. It was well lit by the sun and we could see all its elements very clearly.

Along the equator we communicated with our ocean tracking vessels, the *Akademik Sergei Korolev* and the *Kosmonaut Vladimir Komarov*. We reported that everything was all right; we were 200 m (approx. 650 ft) away from the station. They gave us permission to moor and dock.

We saw the station with the rotating Earth in the background. The sea changed to land and then to mountains. Beautiful.

We docked. There was a signal on the control panel indicating mechanical locking, and the contact bar stretched out toward the station.

"Everything is fine," we reported.

Hurriedly we checked the hermetic seals of the passage hatches and headed toward the station.

We tried to open the hatch of the space vehicle, but we couldn't. I was only able to do this by standing upside-down (an advantage of having no gravity) and pressing my feet against the frame. The hatch finally opened.

The first thought that crossed my mind when we entered the station was that this was going to be our home for the months to come. I was surprised that I didn't recognize it, maybe because I came in at an unusual angle—I walked in on the side panels.

Weightlessness makes everything different. On Earth we get used to everything being on a horizontal or a vertical line. A man walks on the ground, a plant grows up—they're vertical; the Earth's horizon, a flat piece of land—they're horizontal. A man can't walk on Earth upside down or horizontally, but weightlessness allows us to do this here. When we studied the station on the ground, our whole perception of it came from knowing what was up and what was down, where the floor was and where the ceiling was. But in space that doesn't matter. In the same space you can see many different interiors, depending on the position of your body. In other words, it's as though you could imagine several different rooms from one furnished room.

When it was time to sleep, we floated to our sleeping places on the ceiling (that's how we'd thought of it on Earth). I went up to my bed, turned upside down, and stood on it—head down from the Earth's point of view. It wasn't very pleasant, I looked down at the station and forced myself to like the new interior. I tried to reconstruct my image of the station according to my position. Now I think the floor is where my feet are and the ceiling, where my head is. In other words, I am standing on the floor, which was once a ceiling.

When Tolia came over, I told him, "Look what I discovered. Look ahead and you'll see the station looks different, even though we are standing in the normal position."

He said, "That's great, now I'll sleep above you."

"No, you won't," I said. "You'll still sleep on the floor and not on the ceiling, turn upside down again and your bed will still be below." That's how we accepted our unusual situation on the station.

MAY 15

I woke up at 4 a.m. I couldn't sleep, so I assembled an air duct.

Then we spent the whole day, and more, reactivating the station. We worked until 1 a.m. Now we are tired and hungry. I feel okay, but my head hurts. Tolia has already gone to bed. I will too. I can't write anything more than these few lines.

I woke up at eight in the morning. The left side of my forehead hurts, but if I press the back of my head, it helps a little. Tolia is talking in his sleep. My mood is not bad, but if I live with this headache forever, it will drain me completely. Overall I'm up and down all day. In the morning I'm nauseated, but after breakfast my stomach feels better. Work helps, especially when it turns out well. I felt nauseated yesterday and again today when we moved to the station and began to prepare for a TV broadcast. We did plenty of running around, and at the end I got seasick. After that I decided to be more careful. Today we fixed *Delta* (computer complex) and *Rodnik* (water-supply system), and our spirits soared. In the afternoon we did some minor repairs on the cooling-and-drying equipment, which was a pleasure too. Tolia doesn't have a good appetite. I pushed him to eat, but he refused.

"Listen," I told him, "don't spoil *my* appetite. Sit down and eat."

He sat.

The main thing now is to get used to living on our daily schedule. We're still in a state of confusion here, and the schedule must be the basis for our life on board. Tolia and I have a good working relationship—each of us does his own thing and asks the other for help if he needs it.

We heated up and ate freeze-dried food and feel better now. We installed the *Rodnik*, our space water-supply system: it consists of two big containers, holding 250 liters each, located outside the station, in the equipment-assembly compartment. We assembled it according to the instructions, connected the hoses, and now we drink water at our main control post. Now I can sit there and whenever I want to drink, I just turn on the pumping unit and water begins to run. Water tastes good.

On the late-night TV news program, *Vremia*, they called today "the day of active rest." What a joke; we worked all day. At night we cleaned the station and removed a lot of metal scrap. I looked at the Earth when we crossed the terminator. (The terminator is the line separating day from night.—*Ed.*) We were above North America. The lines of the horizon consisted of three or more layers, reminding me of the steps of a pyramid. I am going to sleep now. My head got better by the end of the day.

MAY 17

For the first time I slept as I did on Earth. I feel more relaxed. My head doesn't hurt anymore. Ground Control woke us up and called us to communication. Tolia went on the radio, but I really felt like exercising. I put together the velo-ergometer and then, like a monkey, I turned upside down and began to work with my feet. (Our velo-ergometer is on the ceiling.) I also ran a little bit on the *KTF*, a treadmill. My knees acted up and when I pedaled the bike, they hurt slightly. Running on the treadmill seems to ease the discomfort and improve the circulation to my feet, which often feel very numb. I wanted to run and exert myself.

We received the program for today. It's the second day of station reactivation—I think now our life will gradually begin to take shape.

At 2:06 p.m. we launched the student satellite provided by the Moscow Institute of Aviation. The satellite carries emblems of all the countries that are participants in the *Intercosmos* program. It will be used as an amateur radio repeater station for sending telegrams to the delegates of Nineteenth Komsomol Congress. During the TV broadcast I said that the *Salyut-7* station became a branch of Baikonur on a near-Earth orbit. It is incredible to think that only twenty-five years have passed since the launch of our first satellite into orbit, a major achievement for mankind. Technology has come a long way since then, and now we have student satellites. My country deserves the credit for this. This fact is very symbolic, because the life of society determines the lives and success of our future generations.

After the satellite separation I watched it move away along the left side of the station. As it moved toward the horizon, it looked like a small airplane or glider. Above, the black velvet of space; below, the satellite against the blue aura of Earth's atmosphere. Two side antennas opened; the coils on their tips looked like the wing tanks of an airplane. The hexagonal body of the satellite shone in the sunlight, glittered with its photo-voltaic solar batteries. Beautiful!

Flying at an altitude of 350 km, we look out the portholes and say, "Now this makes all the long training on Earth worthwhile—we could give anything just to see and feel our planet this way."

I am going to sleep, it's late already. Tomorrow we have to wake up early; our day will be very busy. Now we have less time for rest and exercises after lunch. I think that our bodies are adapting, our sleeping pattern has improved, and I feel as good as I did on Earth. It has not taken much time for both of us to adapt to "space" life.

MAY 18

We overslept today and woke up at 9 a.m. Ground Control decided not to wake us up today.

To make them happy, we decided to finish everything they planned for today. Without washing our faces, without shaving, right in our underwear, we started to prepare for the tests of the scientific equipment. We checked the RT-4 X-ray telescope, the BAZK star camera, and the KATE still camera.

Tolia took care of the little things (not that they are any less important), adding additional rubber bands for the attachment of small objects, such as pencils, to secure them in the station. He also attached instruments and set up an additional communication facility in the connecting compartment.

Our meals are cooked by whoever has the time. So, in general, life here is like life in any other new place: you go through an adjustment period; you have to get used to the new house and to a lot of changes. We hid our space suits behind a panel, and the station immediately became roomier.

The day passed quickly because we were working; we do not find enough time to become as familiar with the Earth topography as we should. It is imperative that we become familiar with it, because later during our mission we will need to conduct many visual experiments.

I have a stuffy nose—somewhere I must have sat in a draft. I have been told that this is common here. It is caused by the blood rushing to your head. I exercised on the velo-ergometer, which was lots of fun; I pedaled it with my hands and legs and made up different exercises. That raised my pulse rate to 160, and I wasn't even sweating much.

I watched a thunderstorm above Africa. It was a beautiful view—splashes of lightning, like blooming carnations trembling in the light. They blur and then merge with neighboring flashes, creating a luminous, dancing sea of light in front of the clouds. We passed over the oil fields in Africa—the huge area was illuminated by orange lights. I saw a dark line in the ocean's blue water—I don't know what it could be. I'll have to ask somebody about it. Tomorrow will be a difficult day. Time to sleep.

Book Four of the Bantam Air and Space Series, DIARY OF A COSMONAUT: 211 Days in Space by Valentin Lebedev will be on sale in August 1990 wherever Bantam Books are sold.